Judging Addicts

9/13

R. Smith

Judging Addicts

Drug Courts and Coercion in the Justice System

Rebecca Tiger

NEW YORK UNIVERSITY PRESS
New York and London

NEW YORK UNIVERSITY PRESS
New York and London
www.nyupress.org

References to Internet websites (URLs) were accurate at the time of writing.
Neither the author nor New York University Press is responsible
for URLs that may have expired or changed since the manuscript was prepared.

LIBRARY OF CONGRESS CATALOGING-IN-PUBLICATION DATA
Tiger, Rebecca.
Judging addicts : drug courts and coercion in the justice system / Rebecca Tiger.
p. cm.
Includes bibliographical references and index.
ISBN 978-0-8147-8406-8 (cl : alk. paper)
ISBN 978-0-8147-8407-5 (pb : alk. paper)
ISBN 978-0-8147-5941-7 (ebook)
ISBN 978-0-8147-8596-6 (ebook)
1. Drug courts—United States. 2. Duress (Law)—United States. 3. Drug abuse—
Treatment—Law and legislation—United States. 4. Drug addicts—Legal status, laws, etc.—
United States. I. Title.
KF3890.T54 2012
345.7302770269—dc23   2012024946

New York University Press books are printed on acid-free paper,
and their binding materials are chosen for strength and durability.
We strive to use environmentally responsible suppliers and materials
to the greatest extent possible in publishing our books.

Manufactured in the United States of America
c 10 9 8 7 6 5 4 3 2 1
p 10 9 8 7 6 5 4 3 2 1

For Richard Schoenwald, who taught me how to ask questions

Contents

ACKNOWLEDGMENTS

THIS BOOK WAS long in the making, and it reflects the help of many people who pushed me to think critically about drugs, addiction, and society—and people who made my life fun amid the work.

The late Robert Alford was instrumental in pushing me to articulate the "contradictory institutional logics" that I witnessed in my public health work. When Bob died in 2003, the world lost an amazing sociologist and exemplary mentor. My thinking has been stamped with his unique and critical approach to the social world. Barbara Katz Rothman was the dream adviser; she agreed to oversee a project about which she knew little but still managed to push me to focus on the knowledge that made coerced treatment possible. Barbara has also become a good friend, and she still lets me call on her regularly for advice. Bill Kornblum and Michael Jacobson both enthusiastically supported this research. Bill encouraged me to be clear and Michael, as always, to articulate this project's "so what?" John Torpey pushed me to view this project historically. Without my regular conversations with John about the history of punishment and discipline, I don't think I would have figured out the answer to Michael's persistent question. Carroll Seron enthusiastically discussed my project with me, and provided much-needed encouragement. CUNY Graduate Center generously supported my research.

I was fortunate to receive a fellowship from the National Institute on Drug Abuse that funded me. Many people involved with this fellowship at the National Development and Research Institutes provided invaluable feedback on my work. Greg Falkin and the late Bruce Johnson consistently supported me during my five years in the program. Other fellows wholeheartedly encouraged my critical approach to coerced treatment, and without them, I don't think I would have finished this project. Dina Perrone, in particular, provided much-needed intellectual and emotional support. She still does. Conversations with Rebecca DeGuzman confirmed that "critical addiction studies" does matter; I am thankful for the compatibility of our worldviews. Azure Thompson's astute critiques of my writing certainly strengthened mine. I am always inspired by conversations with Kerwin Kaye, whose stellar research with people coerced into drug treatment pushed me to think more critically about many of my book's conclusions.

My transition to Middlebury College (and life in Vermont) was eased by colleagues who are now also good friends. Laurie Essig generously read the entire manuscript and was instrumental in pushing me to see my book's main points. The amount of time Laurie and Linus Owens devoted to helping me edit this book went way beyond what I could have hoped for from new friends. *Project Runway* cocktail nights with Linus and Penny Evans were also the perfect respite from work. Peggy Nelson's mentoring and friendship continues to be a much-valued source of support for me; regular conversations with her inspire my teaching and research. Start-up funds from Middlebury College allowed me to finish my research and complete the manuscript. Students in my punishment, deviance, and drugs classes have pushed me to clarify many of the ideas I write about here; I am thankful for their enthusiasm for my teaching and research.

Several friends provided the breaks I needed from the single-mindedness of research and writing. Regular dinners with Lynn Horridge were the highlight of my week for several years; Lynn has been one of my most steadfast friends throughout this project. Poker nights with Diana Rickard were always fun, even as we talked about our shared interests in deviance. Visits to Jolene Beiser and Tina Gauthier in California and China reminded me that a world exists outside academia. I am eternally thankful to Julie Netherland and Jessie Daniels, whose hospitality (and perfect martinis) always makes me feel welcome when I return to my home in New York City. And I am grateful to Peter Bruno for helping me feel more at home every day in Vermont.

Over the course of this research, three people who give me immeasurable joy came into my life. I look forward to regular visits with my nieces Eva and Lily and my nephew Jack, and even more so now that I can answer "yes" when they ask if I'm *ever* going to finish my book. My family—Eva, Lily, Jack, Mary, David, Paul, and my parents—provided the support I needed to complete this book.

Ilene Kalish, my editor at NYU Press, expressed nothing but enthusiasm for this project and was a pleasure to work with. Aiden Amos kept me on task, especially when my mind was elsewhere. I am extremely grateful for the anonymous reviewers whose detailed, insightful, and supportive comments strengthened my book.

Finally, although I end up critiquing coerced treatment, I want to thank the people who generously agreed to speak with me about their work on drug courts. In fact, this work would not be possible without them.

Introduction

FIFTEEN YEARS AGO, while riding the NYC subway, I picked up *The New York Times* sitting on the seat next to me and was immediately struck by the article "A Drug Court Takes a Risk to Aid Addicts."[1] It spoke about the emergence of drug courts as a strategy for dealing with nonviolent drug offenders, and referred to the "human resilience" these courts tapped into and their "redemptive possibilities." Brooklyn's district attorney described them as a "symbol of an enlightened answer to the drug plague." Addicts were given the choice of prison or drug treatment; if they chose the latter, they would attend treatment and regularly meet with a judge who had the power to send them to prison if they failed, but this program also gave them the chance to be "clean," productive members of society. This made good sense to me. Addicts needed help, treatment was the best option, and coerced treatment showed that the courts cared about them. And I teared up at the story of Eddie Santiago, with the help of a judge, picking up the pieces of a life destroyed by addiction. As New York State Chief Justice Judith Kaye has explained, these courts fix "ruined lives, broken families, neglected children, ravaged communities."[2] Who could disagree with this?

Drug courts offer a policy approach to drug use that has broad political appeal. Bill Clinton's "drug czar," General Barry McCaffrey, was a vocal supporter of drug courts and oversaw their expansion. George W. Bush praised them as "effective and cost-efficient." And Barack Obama's drug czar, Gil Kerlikowske, is making them a central feature in the Office of National Drug Control Policy's platform. Drug courts have been implemented in every state and have been incorporated into mainstream criminal justice practice. Moving from a small experiment in a few urban areas, drug courts are becoming a central part of the criminal justice system. They are the subject of frequent opinion pieces, praised for their acknowledgment that addiction is a disease best addressed with a combination of treatment and sanctions.[3] A "firm hand" and "swift response to infractions" can be the "best medicine for people with addictions."[4] Rock stars such as Trey Anastasio, the lead singer of Phish, and Slash, the former guitarist of Guns N' Roses, as well as conservative politicians and retired military generals, sing their praises. *Newsweek* recently heralded them a "vanishingly rare thing in Washington: an issue with near consensus."[5] Few people openly critique drug courts, and when they do, they quickly offer suggestions for improving them.[6] The *paradigm* of coerced treatment is rarely questioned; the ideology of drug courts, with its premise that habitual substance use is caused by the disease of addiction, the cure for which is abstinence from drugs best achieved through heavily monitored drug treatment, is now widespread.

The popularity of drug courts rests on hegemonic beliefs about the improvability of the human condition; behavioral flaws stem from diseases that can be diagnosed and fixed. They also draw on our belief that transgressors must be punished even if an underlying disorder is compelling one's deviance. They constitute a seemingly inconsistent marriage of our faith in punishment and treatment, and yet they make perfect sense when we view the development of our ideas about deviance and deviants from a historical perspective. *Judging Addicts* is the story of this development. It focuses on the *ideas* that motivate the practice of coerced drug treatment in the criminal justice system, fully articulated during the Progressive Era in the United States when they were codified in court practice, but predating this institutionalization. I frame these ideas as historical triumphs, rather than scientific ones, and detail their origins. Unlike studies that have ably depicted the inner working of drug courts, their punitive and therapeutic balancing act in the "theater" of the courtroom,[7] I explore how the ideas motivating their practice, as articulated by the words and writings of proponents for coerced treatment, are informed by competing theories of deviance (one viewing it as a crime, the other as an illness), different ideas about how to fix these problems (punishment or treatment), and the overlap between the punitive and medical paradigms. Framed within the sociology of knowledge and a constructionist perspective on social problems, I focus on how the people designing criminal justice policy talk about the problems of drugs and crime, and I attend to the ideas that motivate policy and practice.

Putting Ideas into Practice

My interest in the ideas motivating drug and criminal justice policy developed out of my public health work, where I was actively involved in articulating the disease model of addiction. For several years, I worked as a public health researcher and policy analyst for both city government and nonprofit research organizations in New York City and New Orleans. Much of my work centered around drug policy in the United States, focusing specifically on advancing public health and medicalized perspectives of persistent substance use. Many of the program directors and policymakers I worked with shared a similar perspective—namely, that the correct way to understand persistent substance use, called addiction, was to view it as a disease. Steeped in this framework, I wrote reports and book chapters about substance users and drug policy. In one such chapter, "The Public Policy Context of Drug Use in New York City," my coauthor and I wrote, "Substance abuse is a manageable, chronic disease, not unlike asthma or diabetes. This perspective is informed by a vast body of research on the biomedical bases of addiction."[8] We did not provide any citations to justify this perspective precisely because public health researchers and advocates so widely shared and repeated it as truth.

How did I know persistent substance use was a disease called addiction? Well, in fact, I didn't. However, what I did know, from working with doctors and drug treatment providers, was that the disease model of addiction was considered an enlightened and progressive approach to understanding habitual substance use. Enlightened, because it reflected biomedical and scientific interpretations of deviant behavior. Progressive, because the medical model held the promise of removing the stigma associated with substance use. If addicts were sick, we couldn't blame them for their addiction. And if they were sick, we couldn't punish them for it either. As a participant observer in the world of public health and drug policy, I thought I understood the liberatory implications of this medical framework. I assumed that the adoption of the medical paradigm by the criminal justice system was progress and an important acknowledgment that addicts needed treatment not punishment, that habitual substance use was a medical not criminal justice issue.

Creeping Doubts

But as I started to do more research on drug policy across the country, talking with physicians who treated drug users and ran drug treatment programs and with the people in these programs, many of them poor and black or Latino, the implications of coerced drug treatment started to take on new meaning for me. I discovered that many, and oftentimes most, of the people in drug treatment were mandated there through the criminal justice system regardless of whether they viewed themselves as addicts, and that they were monitored by medical doctors and the court system, by probation or parole officers, and by treatment staff. The data on admissions to drug treatment programs in the United States bear these observations out: the criminal justice system is the largest single source of referrals to publicly funded drug treatment for adults, young adults, and youth.[9] I began to see firsthand how this merger of the punitive and medical produced programmatic and therapeutic contradictions and increased oversight for people trying to please the myriad treatment and criminal justice staff overseeing them. Treatment staff had their decisions second-guessed by judges, many of whom were setting the terms for what "success" in treatment meant. Drug users learned to play the part of contrite addict, deferring to the therapeutic discourse of treatment and the punitive overtones of the court. Treatment providers told drug users that they were sick with the disease of addiction. And yet they were also regularly reminded they were bad. Routine drug testing often led to termination from the program if these tests detected the ingestion of illegal drugs. Security guards stationed by the front door of the treatment program eyed them suspiciously. Reports back to judges and probation officers reminded drug users that people with the power to punish were watching them. Through subtle and overt signs, drug users were reminded that they might be sick with a disease but they were also bad and this badness manifested itself in their drug use.

As someone who believed in and advocated the disease model of addiction, I wondered: If these people were sick, why did the courts have any sustained interest in them? How could they justify this, in the face of the proliferating medical theories of addiction? What happened to the promise of reducing the stigma of substance use by calling it a disease? And did calling something a disease actually reduce stigma?

Working through the Doubts

Judging Addicts stems from these core concerns about the origins and implications of theories of deviance. I examine how drug users are constructed as bad and sick, as bad because they're sick, as always sick and therefore always bad, always within the purview of the criminal justice system. I consider medicine and punishment as important ideological vehicles for advancing the social control of drug users. I frame the medical and punitive perspectives as complementary rather than contradictory approaches to drug use.

My central interests are the forces outside the criminal justice system that provide the basis for the theories about drug use, addiction, and recovery that drug court advocates draw on to construct and justify a role for the courts in solving the complex phenomenon of habitual substance use. I look at how the problem of drug use and its connection to crime is constructed in the first place. Drug courts emerged at a historical moment where institutional crises, such as prison overcrowding, necessitated conceptual transformations in the classification of a group of offenders whose transgressions were drug-related. While still called defendants, these offenders are simultaneously labeled as addicts as well as clients, consumers, and participants. They are both bad and sick, and they are sick with a disease that is both biological and behavioral. Because addicts are sick with a disease that is known through behavioral abnormalities, in this instance criminal conduct, the court is focused on ameliorating these abnormalities. But the goals of drug courts extend far beyond the behavior that led to someone's initial arrest.

Drug courts are predicated on the notion that every aspect of a person's life is affected by their addiction, and thus broad swaths of their lives need to be addressed by the court to intervene in this addiction. Drug court proponents did not construct these theories of addiction; they have been developed and refined for more than two hundred years as a medical model of persistent substance use that viewed addiction as an incurable disease developed. These models hold that addicts have a chronic illness, one that can be managed but never eradicated. It can never be "cured" because addiction is a relapsing condition. Relapse is "inevitable," as so many drug court advocates told me, echoing the now commonplace notion that it is extremely difficult to stop using drugs and that several attempts are necessary for drug users to achieve sobriety—a tenuous sobriety, however, precisely because of the nature of their disease. If relapse is always a possibility, then addicts can never be cured.

Because sobriety is tenuous and abstinence hard to maintain, addicts need help to "stay the course." Drug treatment works but it can't keep addicts there if they don't want treatment or if they seek to stop using drugs through other means. The dominant perspective in the field of addiction treatment and medicine is that, because addiction is a disease, it requires a therapeutic intervention. And because addicts relapse, this intervention needs to be sustained.

Drug courts enter into this discussion, drawing on prevailing medicalized theories to justify the practice of coercing people into drug treatment. But they also add to these medicalized theories of persistent substance use through their consistent advocacy for coercion as the key to effective treatment. They argue that coercion compels addicts to stay in treatment longer than they might if they can enter and leave voluntarily. Drug court advocates actively construct a solution to the problem of addiction that clearly articulates coercion as the centerpiece. The way to achieve this coercion is through the courts, where judges are given the power to both heal and punish. They heal by coercing addicts into drug treatment, with incentives such as reduced prison sentences, and they punish by imposing sanctions, such as periodic incarceration. But this punishment is viewed as part of the healing process, rather than counter to it. Periodic incarceration or other less severe sanctions become the way the court supports the defendant's recovery process.

A second way courts support recovery is by recognizing that the defendant coming through the courts, labeled an addict, is more than just someone who needs to stop using drugs. They are someone whose life is "out of control," as evidenced by repeated arrests, and someone, therefore, who needs help in areas of their life not considered, through strict legal reckoning, within the court's purview. In the name of helping people and facilitating recovery, drug courts expand the scope of activities the court monitors. Rather than punishing a specific act that has happened in the past, drug courts use this specific act—the reason for the person's arrest—as the "opportunity" to affect the defendant's future actions. The court concerns itself with a host of factors in the defendant's life. They justify this expansion through theories of addiction that view habitual substance use as affected by and affecting every aspect of the person's life. Because the addict's behavior also affects other people, conceptualized as "the community," this expansion into increasing aspects of the defendant's life is enacted in the name of public safety.

Drug court advocates explain this increased oversight of defendants with a logic of caring and concern for the lives of defendants. Traditional criminal processing of drug offenders has filled prisons but done nothing to stop drug use or drug-related crimes. Often called "alternatives to incarceration," drug courts are viewed by their advocates as a "revolution-ary" approach, one that injects a "healing" function in the criminal justice system—and one that demands accountability of defendants while offer-ing them the way to transform their lives according to prevailing medical-ized and behavioral theories of addiction and recovery. As C. West Hud-dleston, the CEO of the National Association of Drug Court Professionals, recently wrote, "Drug court clients and professionals alike embody and are shining examples of the courage to make progress every day."[10] Proponents of these courts actively produce a narrative of their noble approach, one that is echoed in the glowing news coverage they receive.

When I originally started this research, I understood drug courts as their proponents presented them, as a "radical reorientation" away from the exclusively punitive approach that had come to dominate contempo-rary punishment. Unlike drug court proponents, and counter to my ini-tially positive response to them, I was concerned by the increasing, and seemingly unprecedented, levels of interaction between the criminal jus-tice and treatment systems I witnessed in my public health work. Drug court advocates genuinely believe that what they are doing is a radical de-parture and that their efforts at rehabilitation differ from previous genera-tions' with the explicit "responsibility" that is foisted on the defendants to be active participants in their own cure. They also believe that their efforts to show that the courts "care" is a departure from the punitive approach of the criminal justice system, where defendants are processed with little con-cern for their interior lives or the underlying motivation for their criminal behavior.

History Repeats Itself

While drug courts contribute to contemporary theories about and discus-sions of addiction, they are part of a larger historical conversation about how to define, contain, and control deviance. Much that has been written about contemporary punishment traces the origins of these increasingly punitive strategies to the early 1970s, when a shift from a "welfarist" ap-proach to punishment to a "managerial" one occurred.[11] Punishment, ac-cording to these scholars, is no longer about transforming the individual but about managing dangerous populations. In much of the literature, two opposing perspectives are mapped out: repressive versus rehabilitative, punitive versus transformative. And yet these typologies can't fully account for any single punishment strategy, no matter how benign or nefarious it seems at first glance. I have come to understand the interplay between the rehabilitative and repressive: they need each other, at any one historical moment, to serve as an important point of contrast. But rehabilitative or punitive in comparison to what?

As I delved into the extensive history of punishment, I realized that the issues plaguing contemporary punishment have deep historical origins. Punishment and discipline have been integral to the formation of the state; nascent communities used rulemaking and their responses to rule-breaking as a way to establish order.[12] The sociologist Kai Erikson, in his groundbreaking work *Wayward Puritans*, showed how the Puritans used punishment as a way of defining who they were as a community. They also developed knowledge about deviance: what produced it and how to classify it. The Puritans used static categories, not unlike the category of "addict" used by drug court advocates, to label deviants permanently as such. While rulebreakers could be reformed, and reform was an important goal of punishment, their status as deviant remained constant and served as a reminder to the larger community about the rules that were necessary to determine the community's survival. The contradiction in punishment, then, is that it is meant to fix the offender who, because of prevailing theories of deviance, can never fully be fixed.

This tension inherent in punishment reforms, and their inability to fix people, has led to what the historian David Rothman has defined as a cycle of "conscience and convenience" as each generation attempts to get punishment "right."[13] Through his examination of Jacksonian and Progressive Era punishment transformations in the United States, Rothman identified a cycle whereby conscience propelled reformers to transform the status quo of punishment. Armed with new theories about what causes crime and how to fix the individual criminal, these reformers argued for a more humane way to punish transgressors. Prisons, considered by many today to exemplify one of the least humane approaches to punishment, were the result of reformers' efforts and were considered the most progressive and enlightened way to alter behavior. The ideals of the reformers, however noble, are often taken over by the imperatives of convenience, where misapplications of the underlying principles that guided the reform are put in place, partly for institutionally expedient reasons. The misapplication then leads to new reform efforts meant to cure the ills that come out of the previous reformers' efforts.

Progressive Era reformers initiated a host of transformations in punishment that were largely attempts to undo the deleterious effects of the prison and to enact the kind of personal transformation progressives thought was the key to curing deviance and deviants. They emphasized a personalized approach to punishment and heavy judicial discretion, and were convinced this discretion was essential to address the environmental and psychological causes of crime. It was this same personalized approach that would come under attack fifty years later by reformers who argued that discretion led, among other things, to gross abuses of the system and to racial discrepancies in sentencing.

My Argument

Framing drug courts within these broader historical perspectives as well as within contemporary discussions of punishment, deviance, and addiction has led me to revise my original understanding of drug courts' historical uniqueness and to the five main conclusions about drug courts, summarized briefly here, that this book will address.

First, drug courts, rather than constituting a "radical reorientation" or a "triumph of the disease model," are neither radical nor a triumph.[14] Instead, they greatly resemble the Progressive Era reforms that influenced punishment in the late nineteenth and early twentieth centuries. Then, as now, the medical model of deviant behavior was a key tool advocates used to justify court expansion and the individualized punishment/rehabilitation they enacted, rather than to cede control of social problems to the medical establishment. Like these earlier reforms, drug courts draw on outside disciplinary perspectives to articulate an enhanced role for the court as an institution that uses its punitive power to coerce rehabilitation in the name of "helping" people, rather than solely punishing them. In doing so, the advocates of drug courts reform how the criminal justice system understands and responds to drug-related offenses while firmly cementing the control of addiction in the hands of this same system. Drug courts aren't a particular triumph because, even in the most inflated estimate of their scope, they affect a mere fraction of the more than seven million people currently under criminal justice supervision in the United States.

Second, despite the deep historical precedents for coerced treatment, drug court advocates speak, almost uniformly, as if these courts represent a radically new approach to addressing criminal offenders. The advocates I interviewed believe that drug courts are the right way for the criminal justice system to deal with drug users. They see these courts as unprecedented and visionary. Because they speak with an almost monolithic voice about these courts, they do not, with a few exceptions, engage seriously with the critiques that were lodged against, and led in part to the demise of, their Progressive Era predecessor courts. Unquestioningly believing that drug courts are better than prison, and viewing prison as the only other way to deal with drug offenders, the advocates I interviewed dismissed any serious consideration that judges might use their greatly expanded powers in potentially dangerous ways.

Third, the disease designation, while an attempt to differentiate among the individuals under criminal justice supervision, actually obscures their racial homogeneity. By ascribing a disease state to defendants, drug courts erase racial bias from the equation: discussions of race were uniformly absent from my interviews with advocates about coerced treatment and criminal justice processing. The advocates I interviewed spoke about the "revolving door" of drug offenders, the explosion of drug-related arrests in the 1980s, and the jail and prison overcrowding that compelled them to seek alternative sanctions to prison for *addicts*. In a criminal justice system defined almost exclusively in terms of racial inequality, where African Americans and Latinos are vastly overrepresented and far more likely than their white drug-using counterparts to be arrested, the absence of a discussion of race is notable. According to this disease logic, the state of addiction renders individuals vulnerable to criminal justice involvement, not bias in policing, arrest, charging, conviction, and sentencing that leads some drug uses directly into long-term oversight by the criminal justice system. Again, this medicalizing of defendants resembles the Progressive Era reforms where middle-class anxieties about immigrant behavior were translated into disease designations that permitted new forms of social control.

Fourth, by removing consideration of race and class, drug courts continue with rather than depart from the historically persistent efforts to define deviance in ways that are compatible with an implicit logic of inequality, and that complement rather than counter the concentrated institutional context of prison. Drug courts echo the specific concerns of the Progressive Era reformers, with the use of the courts as the site for enacting medical and behavioral sanctions, as well as the broader concerns of control and deviance that predate the Progressive Era. Thus they are a part of the cycle of conscience and convenience as each generation of middle-class reformers attempts to model punishment on prevailing norms and enact social control over "unruly" classes in ways that are compatible with prevailing sensibilities about the causes of and cures for deviance.

Fifth, and overall, understanding punishment from this historical perspective, and the needs it serves in the community, it is difficult, and irrelevant, to declare any one punishment strategy "innovative," "groundbreaking," or any of the many other adjectives that have been used to describe the historically persistent efforts of reformers to craft punishment that "works." The one constant is the need to figure out how to enact effective punishment. Effective *at what* is an issue this book will directly take on, focusing on the ways that drug court advocates stake a claim for the courts in treating such a complex concept as addiction.

While historical considerations are paramount to this book's argument, it is also important to emphasize, as the historical sociologist Philip Gorski points out, that "similar is not identical."[15] Drug and problem-solving courts are emerging at a particular historical time. This historicity affects the theories of crime, addiction, and the court's role in solving social problems that court reformers draw on and construct. It also affects the arguments reformers develop, how they frame these arguments, the way they justify their interventions, and the shape these interventions take. This book is focused on articulating these theories, providing their historical precedents, and considering drug courts as a distinct, yet interconnected, moment in the construction of the problems of deviance, crime, and punishment.

Overview

Chapter 1 provides the background about the history of drug courts and the specific theory and methods I used for this book. In it I discuss the theoretical background for my study's empirical focus, detailing the sociology of knowledge literature. I argue for an approach to understanding punishment that views the construction of the "problems" of crime, punishment, and deviance as an important area of inquiry, an approach that considers the ideas behind drug courts as relevant for understanding their expansion.

Chapter 2 details the history of punishment in the United States. I describe the competing theories that have prevailed throughout the history of punishment about what exactly causes people to transgress norms and what compels them to commit crimes. I link these theories to generalized constructions of deviance as well as specific strategies that have been used to define, contain, and control criminal behavior.

In Chapter 3 I draw on the words and writings of drug court proponents to detail the multiple problems they were responding to when they developed this particular model of coerced treatment. As this chapter shows, drug court advocates were concerned by the increased and repeat incarceration of drug offenders. Their solution was to put rehabilitation back on the agenda of the criminal justice system in a way that rehabilitates the status of judges and the courts while "fixing" defendants. Rather than viewing the decriminalization of drugs as a means to reduce the prison population, they see drug courts as a solution that allows the criminal justice system to regain legitimacy and retain control of drug users. It is here and in chapter 5 that advocates' uniform sentiments about drug courts become apparent.

Because prevailing approaches to punishment are affected by ideas with origins outside punishment, I pay attention in chapter 4 to the rise of medicalized theories of addiction that drug court advocates draw on to stake their claim over addicts. It is these now dominant ideas that are the basis for the broad support for drug courts.

In Chapter 5 I show how drug court advocates draw on the prevailing medical and social sciences to explain addiction and to argue for treatment over incarceration. In doing so, however, they create their own theoretical logic when they argue for the importance of coercion—and especially the role coercion can play in rehabilitating someone who is sick. Drug court advocates merge seemingly contradictory perspectives in making their "case for coercion," and draw on theories of addiction that are heavily influenced by biomedical perspectives to argue for enhanced court and judicial oversight of defendants.

Chapter 6 discusses the future of drug courts, focusing on the recent preoccupation of advocates with these courts' institutionalization. I show how they attempt to balance contradictions that are inherent in efforts to "institutionalize" interventions whose very success is ascribed, by these same advocates, to their highly personal nature. Judges gain personal knowledge about each defendant that can be used to enact consequences that will impress on the defendant the importance of following the pre-scribed treatment protocol. One of the main features of drug courts—their individualized and personalized nature—is in direct tension with the imperatives of institutionalization. This tension is manifested in the advocates' lack of consensus about what drug court success means. I also discuss the expansion of the drug court model, as it moves horizontally to other forms of criminality, redefined as medicalized deviance, and verti-cally, to juveniles who are a renewed target for coercive therapeutic crimi-nal justice measures.

In the book's conclusion, I consider alternatives to drug courts and the criminalization of drugs and drug users that entail neither punitive over-sight nor coercion. Highlighting the contradictions in our drug policy, where some people are punished for using mind-altering substances while others are encouraged to use them via prescription pharmaceuticals, I re-iterate the idea that our preoccupation is less with drug use than with the behavior of certain drug users. I conclude that unless we have an episte-mological shift in how we understand drugs, drug users, the value of sobri-ety, and the role of the state in coercing health, we will continue in a failed cycle with long historical roots and precedents.

"Drug Court Works," claims a bumper sticker sold by the National As-sociation of Drug Court Professionals. Four recent studies suggest the contrary and have leveled critiques against drug courts similar to those that hastened the demise of Progressive Era reforms.[16] They fail to address the racial bias in the criminal justice system and therefore favor white de-fendants, screening out African Americans. They are "conviction mills," forcing people to plead guilty to get into the drug courts. They "widen the net" of the criminal justice system: more rather than fewer people are ar-rested for low-level drug offenses because drug courts are an alternative av-enue through which to process these defendants. They diminish resources for people who want to enter treatment voluntarily, diverting increasingly scarce funds for drug treatment to people mandated there through the criminal justice system. People who fail at drug court and go to prison end up spending more time incarcerated than if they had bypassed drug court altogether.

Judging Addicts is both an intellectual and political enterprise. By attend-ing to and contextualizing how advocates of coerced treatment craft their arguments, I am showing how they are making ideological arguments, framed within the technical language of criminal justice processing, that have broad social resonance. They appeal to prevailing ideas about the connection between drugs and crime, the values of sobriety, and the importance of "doing good" while disciplining. They actively construct force as the best medicine. Can we imagine a world where drug users aren't subjected to medical control and criminal justice coercion?

1

Both Bad and Sick

AN AFRICAN AMERICAN woman in her mid-thirties is escorted into the courtroom, her hands shackled behind her back. She faces the judge. It's already been decided, before she gets there, that she will plead guilty to assault charges. Her sentence will be eighteen months in a lockdown, inpatient drug treatment facility. Her attorney provides the judge with some details of her life. She's been homeless since she was eleven. She's been arrested several times, for prostitution and theft. She's been an addict for over twenty years. The judge repeats the offer of drug treatment, interspersing her legal, formal language with words of encouragement. It's because the court cares and believes she can get better that she is being offered this opportunity. The defendant nods her head vigorously, repeatedly thanking the judge for this chance. The judge reminds her that this is tough work, and that there will be severe consequences if she doesn't follow the treatment program. The defendant continues to nod, promising to do her best. The uniformed guards escort her from the courtroom. Looking back over her shoulder, she repeats "thank you" several times. A member of the drug court clinical staff whom I am sitting next to leans over and whispers to me, "Of course she's going to say yes to drug court. She's been homeless for so long, where else is she going to go?"

Scenes like this are repeated across the country regularly in drug courts. Judges interact with defendants differently than in traditional criminal court. They inquire about children, jobs, romantic relationships, and plans for education, comment on defendants' appearances, or scold them for inappropriate language. They offer a "tough love" approach to defendants, being both judge, with the power to punish, but also a type of "case manager" or "therapeutic administrator."[1] Defendants, also called clients and participants, face the judge, who offers them treatment but forcefully reminds them that it is no substitution for punishment.

The courtroom is an important aspect of drug courts, even though defendants spend the majority of their sentence in drug treatment programs. The sociologist James Nolan, in his ethnography of several drug courts titled *Reinventing Justice: The American Drug Court Movement*, refers to their "theatrical aspects" and "dramaturgical character." Judges praise and admonish defendants, commenting on both small issues and larger infractions that affect the defendant's sentence. A judge might remind the defendant to use "sir" and to speak and look up when addressing the judge. These behavioral comments, a form of discipline, are for the benefit of the particular defendant facing the judge as well as the others present in the courtroom on the day's docket. Judges also respond to infractions of the treatment program, including "dirty urines," the toxicological signs of continued drug use. These personal issues—relapse and continued drug use, the "triggers" that propel the defendant to use drugs—are addressed in the courtroom in front of the other defendants and other members of the "audience." In Nolan's study, judges referred to themselves as both "stage director" and "lead actor." They are performing in the courtroom. As one drug court treatment director explained to Nolan, "It's orchestrated. It's a show. You are putting on a show."[2] The point of the show is to remind everyone in the courtroom of the judge's authority. It is to create a sense of accountability in the defendant, whose actions affect not only themselves but also everyone else in the courtroom, their lives, and the wider community.

In the theater of the courtroom, judges are enacting decisions that have been made behind the scenes, prior to the defendant's face-to-face encounter with the judge, although the latter often acts as if this is the first time he or she is learning the specifics of the defendant's case. The "drug court team," usually comprising the judge, prosecution, defense, probation representative, and a clinical director with drug treatment experience, meet prior to the court session to discuss each case and the defendant–client's progress in treatment. They alert the judge to any developments related to setbacks in treatment and suggest appropriate sanctions. The drug court team members have considerable discretion. If a defendant has "started using" again or engaged in other criminal activity but has been cooperative throughout the process, this information is considered and dealt with before the judge addresses the defendant in the courtroom. Likewise, if the defendant is considered by the drug court team to be difficult, the same infraction that leads to leniency for one defendant could lead to expulsion from the program for another.

Two examples from the recent HBO documentary series *Addiction* featuring the South Boston Drug Court highlight the deliberate nature of this differential treatment and its centrality to how drug courts are represented in the approving media coverage they receive. The nine-part *Addiction* series, a collaboration between HBO, the Robert Wood Johnson Foundation, the National Institute on Drug Abuse (NIDA), and the National Institute on Alcohol Abuse and Alcoholism, is meant to "demystify" addiction and present it as a treatable, chronic brain disease.[3] The *Addiction* series, best understood as an advocacy piece for NIDA's brain model of habitual substance use, was accompanied by an Addiction Project Outreach: the Robert Wood Johnson Foundation funded public health and abstinence-oriented drug treatment and addiction organizations to host viewing parties for the series to ensure that its message reached the widest audience possible. Series segments examining institutional sites where addiction is managed bolstered the overall message that addiction is a treatable, chronic brain disease. The series was widely praised; *The New York Times* lauded it for its "profiles of successful treatment programs" such as drug courts.[4]

This South Boston Drug Court episode opens with handcuffed men getting out of a police van, then immediately moves to a view of the men's bathroom, where a defendant leaves a stall, handing a cup to court staff who have watched him while he urinated in it; it will immediately be tested for drugs. In the next scene, one drug court client, Daniel, explains that he used drugs again but tells the interviewer, who responds with approving verbal encouragement, "Instead of lying and getting caught in the urine, I came up here, I talked to my probation officer. I told him the truth, something I usually don't do. I told him I messed up. It's a vicious cycle." In a subsequent scene, the presiding drug court judge, Robert Zemian, is speaking to Daniel. "Did you figure out what happened?" the judge asks Daniel. "Yeah," Daniel responds. "Yes," the judge corrects him. "I'm just getting real bored with everything," Daniel explains. "It shouldn't be an excuse but I used it as one. I'm back on the beam now." The judge tells Daniel, "You did as well as anyone was doing here. It was very disappointing to me but you reacted correctly, which is important." Daniel is given a probation violation and must go back to visiting the court every two weeks, where he will meet with the judge and resume regular drug testing. Daniel has been deemed sufficiently motivated. We later find out that he has lost his job but will begin working again soon; he's buying a house and recently proposed marriage to his girlfriend. The court has to deal with his "slip"; he expressed enough deference to the process that his relapse is treated as part of, rather than counter to, the therapeutic process.

In contrast, Patrick is trouble for the court. In the pre-court meeting, the drug court team discusses his case. One court staff member tells the judge that she's "having problems with him." The probation officer on the team explains, "What concerns me about this case is that each time he comes back, he comes back with the same complaint. He wants to write his own treatment plan. He's not cooperating." The judge tells the team, "We'll deal with him in court." In court, the judge looks at Patrick and shakes his head disapprovingly. The probation officer explains what he has already told the judge and what the judge already knows: "He's been found in violation of his probation, he went into treatment, tested positive for opiates." The judge tells Patrick, "You did well for periods of time but you've been out there too long and you know what's going to happen. You're going to have to do the program in the house of corrections." Patrick asks if there's a chance that he can move to another program. The judge tells him that "there's always a chance" but remands him to prison, where he remains for six months. He is ultimately denied reentry into drug court.

While both Daniel and Patrick used drugs, Daniel took the blame for his relapse while Patrick attributed it to the treatment program. Daniel's explanation for his drug use fit within the treatment paradigm of the court; Patrick's justification implicitly questioned the efficacy of treatment while simultaneously deferring blame. Daniel also displayed sufficient respect for, and a desire to be a part of, the institutions of work and marriage, portrayed here as a sign that he is engaged in the recovery process. In drug courts, the judge and other court staff are always assessing the defendant's commitment to treatment and amenability to change.[5] It is factors such as these, and the discretion that comes with them, that are used to determine a drug court client's fate.

Judges also reacquaint themselves with the specifics of a defendant's case so that when they face the defendant in the courtroom, they can enact the personalized nature of drug courts, considered essential to their success. The judge can show that he or she cares about the defendant and remembers important details of the defendant's life. Drug courts collect very personal information on defendants, which is considered essential to the courts' success. The sociologists Stacey Burns and Mark Peyrot, in their ethnography of a two drug courts in Southern California, emphasize the dual nature of this personalized information. Its goal is to convey caring, to show that the court is committed to the defendant's recovery, but it is also a way that defendants are held accountable to the court. It is part of the "mentoring and monitoring" function of the drug court. The individualized information that judges collect can be used to craft meaningful rewards but also particularly effective sanctions. The personal information, combined with strict monitoring, is used to determine a defendant's progress in the drug courts, measured in stages. These stages, ranging from the trial orientation phase to graduation, can take years for a defendant to complete. As the defendant progresses through these stages, the monitoring becomes less intense. They can also be demoted back to earlier stages if they do not comply with treatment. During these stages, the judge often uses jail as an "extension of recovery" and a form of "behavior modification." As one judge they interviewed explained, sanctions are "supposed to put that kind of torture and fear and whatever else is unpleasant in your memory so that when you do cross that trigger again, you really remember. . . . The behavior modification thing . . . is basically pleasure and pain."[6]

An important aspect to drug courts is that judges show they care about defendants. They recommend sanctions for "dirty urines." They take into account participants' commitment to sobriety. Judges praise, cajole, reprimand, and lecture drug court participants. Sometimes they hug them. They remind them that sobriety is difficult to achieve but that actions, such as "slip-ups," have consequences. The judge is there to remind them of these consequences, which can range from courtroom admonishments to brief stints in jail to years in prison. These consequences remind defendants that they are in control. They might be sick with a disease, a compulsive relationship with drugs, but its cure rests within them and their commitment to the hard work of sobriety. Some defendants, unable to convince the judge of this commitment, end up in prison. Having pled guilty to get into the drug court, they have a certain prison sentence waiting for them when they fail to achieve sobriety.

Background

Formed partly in response to the overcrowding of jails and prisons that has stemmed from punitive drug policies, drug courts are intended to address the underlying addiction many in the criminal justice system believe is the impetus for crime while retaining the coercion traditionally associated with criminal justice.[7] As the U.S. Department of Justice's Drug Courts Program Office explains, "Drug courts leverage the coercive power of the criminal justice system to achieve abstinence and alter criminal behavior through the combination of judicial supervision, treatment, drug testing, incentives, sanctions and case management."[8] Unlike previous attempts at coerced treatment, sanctions "of increasing severity"—including incarceration—imposed by the judge are considered "instrumental" in drug court operation.[9] Drug court judges retain considerable power over the treatment process, meet regularly in the courtroom with defendants, and routinely monitor their progress, using urine testing and reports from treatment programs to assess compliance with treatment protocol.[10]

Since their first appearance in Dade County, Florida, in 1989, drug courts have expanded to every state, with 2,459 in operation as of December, 2009.[11] The majority of these, 1,317, are for adult felony offenders, 455 are for juveniles, and more than 300 are family drug courts. It is difficult to get consistent data on the number of people who have gone through drug courts. According to the National Association of Drug Court Professionals (NADCP), the sole drug court advocacy organization in the United States, more than 300,000 people have "participated" in drug courts since 1989; however, the organization does not provide any data on completion rates for these people.[12] NADCP estimated that, as of December 2008, there were over 116,000 drug court participants and that over 22,000 people graduated successfully in 2008. I could find no data on the numbers of people who did not complete the drug court program. NADCP claims, on their website, that "drug courts transform over 120,000 addicts yearly in adult, juvenile, and family court systems into drug-free, productive citizens."[13] The discrepancy between 22,000 graduates, 116,000 participants, and 120,000 lives transformed is too large to begin to estimate the real numbers of people graduating from drug courts in any one year, and speaks to the difficulty in discussing, with any accuracy, a punishment strategy whose main source of data collection and reporting is also its advocacy organization. Added to this, many judges not presiding over drug courts mandate people to drug treatment.

Drug courts come in two main models: pre-plea and post-plea. In pre-plea drug courts, also called "deferred prosecution," the defendant enters mandated drug treatment before pleading guilty to a charge. If the defendant completes treatment, the charges are dismissed. If the defendant doesn't complete treatment, she or he is then prosecuted for the original offense. According to the U.S. General Accounting Office, this pre-plea model "is intended to capitalize on the trauma of arrest" to get people into treatment with the possibility of avoiding a felony conviction.[14] In the post-plea model, the defendant pleads guilty to the offense before accessing drug treatment. The sentence is suspended or deferred while the defendant is in treatment. But because they have pled guilty to a felony, which carry strict sentencing guidelines, they have a certain prison sentence awaiting them if they do not complete the treatment program. If they successfully complete the treatment program, their sentences are waived or, in some instances, their case records are expunged.

As the GAO explains of the pre- and post-plea models, "Both of these approaches provide the offender with a powerful incentive to complete the requirements of the drug court program,"[15] the incentive being an almost certain prison sentence if they fail to complete drug treatment. While drug courts initially started with a pre-plea model, 58% of adult drug courts are now post-plea.[16] This means that the majority of drug court participants, in order to access drug courts, have pled guilty to a felony and will face the charges for this felony if they do not comply with court-mandated treatment.

An important component to the expansion of drug courts, since the early 1990s when there were fewer than twenty, has been their inclusion in federal criminal justice policy. The Omnibus Crime Control and Safe Streets Act of 1994's Title I, Subchapter XII-J, authorized the attorney general to make federal dollars available to states, local governments, and court systems to establish drug courts.[17] In many jurisdictions, drug courts have been incorporated into state court systems and are funded through state criminal justice channels rather than through federal technical assistance or start-up grants.[18] Some states are using the drug court model of coerced treatment, intensive supervision, and sanctions in other specialized courts such as mental health, juvenile justice, domestic violence, reentry, tribal, family dependence, gambling, and truancy courts.[19]

The Obama administration strongly supports drug courts as part of its "demand-side" approach to drug policy. The new drug czar, Gil Kerlikowske, has explained that the Obama administration will focus much of its drug control strategy on prevention and treatment and is moving away from the language of the "War on Drugs."[20] Obama recently almost doubled the allocation for drug courts, from $25 million to $45 million, through the Department of Justice. Kerlikowske, a former police officer who served as Seattle's chief of police for eight years, has said that "we need to approach the drug problem as a disease, not a crime problem."[21]

Despite this rhetoric of an emphasis on treatment, Obama has made little movement toward changing the overall framework of the War on Drugs; he has not called for the legalization of drugs or the dismantling of the war's underlying premise. His most recent drug policy budget bears striking similarities to George W. Bush's, with twice as much money going to the criminal justice system than to drug treatment and prevention.[22] This makes sense when we view the expansion of drug courts as part of the criminalization of drug users: treatment is offered once the criminal justice system becomes involved.

All Rise

The National Association of Drug Court Professionals, perhaps emboldened by Obama's stated support but also the seemingly nonpartisan faith in coerced treatment, has begun a new campaign called All Rise to advocate for increased funding for drug courts. All Rise's tagline is "Restoring Lives, Reuniting Families, and Making Communities Safer."[23] C. West Huddleston, NADCP's CEO, explained recently in *The Huffington Post* that "whenever one person rises of out of addiction and crime, we all rise as a community. When a child is reunited with clean and sober parents, we all rise. When the intergenerational cycle of drug addiction in a family is broken and healing begins, we all rise."[24] The responses to this *Huffington Post* piece and drug courts generally were uniformly glowing. Drug court judges, treatment providers, and graduates posted responses to the story speaking to the "sanity" of the drug court model amid the insanity of the criminal justice system. The consensus was that treatment works and prison doesn't; drug courts are the perfect solution to the drug problem. One drug court staff member wrote in the comments section, "Only the church has the greater opportunity to produce meaningful lasting change than do these courts." The opinion, widely shared, was that drug courts are the only other alternative to incarceration.

Drug Court Evaluations

The idea that drug courts "work" has become widespread and oft repeated in their glowing newspaper coverage. According to *The New York Times*, these courts, "where emotions are on the surface . . . are one of the few initiatives that reduce recidivism . . . and save taxpayer money."[25] While acknowledging that a large percentage of participants drop out of drug courts, potentially compromising the findings of "success" among those who stay in, the article finishes with a focus on the important role a judge can play in helping people "straighten out." Another *New York Times* article, "Court Treatment System Is Found to Help Drug Offenders Stay Clean," repeats this idea that drug courts work, despite acknowledging that some people are actually worse off after having attended drug courts.[26] The positive coverage of drug courts focuses on individual cases to highlight the courts' success—Allison is reunited with her daughter, Jimmie has stayed clean for a year, Bonnie is thankful for the arrest that allowed her to break her addiction to cocaine, Scott is now drug-free and getting married.[27] The success is the personal stories where people volunteer to participate in drug courts, struggle through their recovery with judges who often jail them for dirty urines, and emerge clean and committed to sobriety to fulfill their social obligations as worker, parent, and spouse. We hear of addicts who are *thankful* for arrests, of judges who *care* about defendants, of courtrooms overflowing with tough love and heightened emotions. They "salvage nonviolent addicts before they harden into predatory criminals";[28] support for these courts is based on this widespread belief that addiction and criminality are virtually synonymous.

Newspaper coverage of drug court success often draws on evaluations of these courts to bolster their claims that judicially monitored mandated treatment works. These evaluations are an important part of the ideological success of drug courts; they use quantitative data to back up this widespread belief that habitual substance use is a form of sickness and badness, best managed through a combination of treatment and force. The Center for Court Innovation, one of the most important court and criminal justice reform organizations in the United States, has conducted several studies of drug courts; an analysis of these reports reveals the assumptions about drug use and addiction underlying these courts. My discussion of these evaluations is not meant to serve as an exhaustive meta-analysis of drug court outcomes. Rather, I focus on a few prominent evaluations, whose findings were widely reported, to highlight how these are used to help confirm the assumption that drug courts work by setting, in part, the framework for how to think about and evaluate coerced treatment. I am focusing on these evaluations as an important part of the knowledge construction of drug courts, displaying in their seemingly neutral empirical language the ideology of addiction on which drug courts are predicated.

One such report, titled "Drug Courts an Effective Treatment Alternative," explains that these courts address "addiction-driven crime" and are fueled by the "largely intuitive belief in the power of treatment."[29] But they are not just based on the (unproved) idea that treatment works, but also that the *longer* one stays in treatment the better: if some treatment is good, then more must be better. These evaluations, then, are structured to confirm this "intuitive belief" that lengthy stays in treatment are more effective than shorter ones. One Center for Court Innovation evaluation of eleven drug courts in New York State found that in eight of these courts, 60% of drug court participants either graduated or were still in treatment after one year.[30] They compared this to data on people who voluntarily entered inpatient treatment and found that "just" 10–30% were still in treatment after one year. This fact—that some drug court participants stay in treatment longer than those who are there voluntarily—is translated into the empirical claim that drug courts therefore must be more effective than voluntary treatment because longer stays in treatment are "better." All we really know is that people who stay in treatment longer spend more time in treatment. Here we see the ideological faith that treatment cures addiction translated into a certainty that drug courts work. The question remains: if these courts are supposed to be a *criminal justice* innovation, why are they using people in *drug treatment* as their comparison group? By doing so, they are confirming the idea that coerced treatment is better than voluntary treatment and expanding their jurisdiction as both a punitive and therapeutic innovation.

The Center for Court Innovation evaluations have also focused on comparisons with defendants not participating in drug courts. They found, in New York State, that six of eleven drug courts studied reduced reconviction rates by 29% over three years after initial arrest. One is left wondering what the results were in the other five courts they studied. They conclude that drug court graduates are most likely not to reoffend but provide no data for how many defendants in the eleven courts they studied actually graduated. "Drug courts work," the evaluators conclude. "This study arguably offers a new level of confidence in the positive nature of the drug court intervention . . . [and] supports further replication of drug courts."[31]

The assumption that "drug courts work" is widespread among advocates of these courts—many of whom are also their evaluators. The assumed success of drug courts is the starting point for a more recent report by the Center for Court Innovation titled "The State of Drug Court Research: Moving Beyond 'Do They Work?'" This certainty that drug courts do indeed work, combined with their expansion based partly on this premise, has "spawned an urgent set of second-generation questions focusing less on *whether* drug courts work and more on *how* and *for whom*, along with *how they might work better*."[32] The authors describe these as "action research questions" that "focus less on evaluating bottom-line success and more on providing feedback that can improve everyday program quality."[33] Again, the assumption is that drug courts work; we can now move beyond the question of their effectiveness and focus on ways to help them work better. Despite acknowledging that much of the evaluation literature on drug courts has been "plagued by methodological issues necessitating the careful interpretation of many drug court studies," the authors conclude, again, that longer treatment is better, that drug court participants stay in treatment longer, and that the key to this "success" is, in part, "the legal pressure entailed by the threat of incarceration drug court participants face in the event of failure; several studies confirm that legal coercion is a sizable force improving both short-term and long-term treatment outcomes."[34] The ideology that addiction is a disease best managed through coerced treatment is confirmed by these findings, in part because they assume, rather than interrogate, this "intuitive belief" that treatment works.

The idea that coerced treatment works hinges on a belief that graduated sanctions, including periodic jail time, are the key to drug court effectiveness. And yet, as an "alternative to incarceration," as their advocates call them, "drug courts typically aspire to reduce the time that defendants spend in jail or prison."[35] Despite this, some evaluations have found that drug court participants spend more time in jail than comparison groups as "an intermediate sanction for noncompliant behavior." In three of six drug courts studied in New York State, drug court defendants spent the same or more amount of time in jail than the control group. These findings suggest a large flaw in the drug court model as an *alternative* to incarceration. And yet, even this finding, perhaps the most devastating to their alternative claims, is explained thus: "Of course, since drug courts reduce recidivism, it is likely that if including incarceration time served as a result of new offenses, most drug courts would ultimately achieve reductions in net jail or prison time."[36] Here, the seemingly negative finding—that some drug court participants spend equal or more time in jail than they would have if they had bypassed drug courts—is justified within the unshakable framework that "drug courts work." The assumption is that without drug court, defendants would be rearrested and incarcerated, so even extra jail time while in drug court is excused; without drug court, the defendant would undoubtedly face future incarceration.

Recent evaluations of drug court evaluations stand in stark contrast to the positive reports presented by their evaluator–advocates. A recent meta-analysis of drug court studies, funded by the Drug Policy Alliance, summarizing the results of the five-year Multi-site Adult Drug Court Evaluation, explains that drug court participation did not lead to a statistically significant reduction in rearrest, despite the strong claims for this finding in the Center for Court Innovation's studies. Further, this report claims that "incarceration sanctions"—considered by many advocates to be an important component of drug court success—are associated with a lower probability of program completion, in part because "a person's sense of autonomy and motivation—integral to progress in treatment—can be undermined if they feel they are sanctioned unfairly."[37] Further, some reports suggest that drug courts have not reduced, and in some places have actually increased, incarceration for drug offenses. In some jurisdictions, defendants who start but do not complete drug court may face longer sentences than if they had bypassed drug court altogether. With completion rates ranging from 30% to 70% nationally, this suggests that a significant number of one-time drug court participants will end up incarcerated. Combined with the use of jail as a "treatment tool," drug courts' claim as an alternative to incarceration is called into question with these findings.

War on Drugs

How did we get to this place where people see coerced drug treatment with the threat of incarceration as an enlightened and humane approach to drug use? The escalating punitiveness of drug policy in the United States helps explain, in part, the positive support drug courts have received. The increasing criminalization of drug use over the past forty years, as evidenced by lengthy mandatory sentences for drug convictions and dramatic increases in federal funding for the War on Drugs, has had a significant impact on the number of people incarcerated in the United States, which now exceeds 2.3 million.[38] Of the 5.1 million additional people under criminal justice supervision, the majority is regularly drug tested and must remain drug-free as a condition of their probation or parole.[39] During the same time that arrests of drug users have been escalating, research into the etiology of the "disease" of addiction has received considerable attention by the scientific and medical community and funding from the federal government.[40] Most medical and behavioral theories of addiction view it as a compulsive behavior amenable to treatment, even though these theories are often in conflict about the nature of addiction. The therapeutic and criminalized perspectives are seemingly contradictory approaches to the "problem" of substance use, with one calling for treatment and the other punishment. Despite these contradictions, these perspectives merge with the use of coerced drug treatment as a punishment for drug-related offenses.

Coerced Treatment

While the U.S. government experimented throughout the twentieth century with different policy approaches to drug use, concerted efforts to coerce drug users into treatment as a criminal justice strategy began in earnest in the early 1960s. California's Civil Addict Program, implemented in 1961 and run by the Department of Corrections, permitted the state to involuntarily commit people for several years of inpatient drug treatment and follow-up. In 1966 the federal government passed the Narcotic Addict Rehabilitation Act, which permitted all states to implement coerced treatment programs.[41] In most states, treatment services were provided in prison settings, yet funds from this act helped establish a system of drug treatment programs that was virtually nonexistent before this time. Treatment Alternatives to Street Crime, developed in the 1970s and still in existence, was the first major coerced treatment program that took drug offenders out of the criminal adjudication process and placed them in drug treatment facilities not run by the criminal justice system.[42] Defendants were returned to the court system when they had completed treatment, but they had little interaction with judges during treatment.

Despite the lengthy history of the relationship between the criminal justice and drug treatment systems, this connection had been sporadic and efforts were stymied by the increasing use of incarceration to punish drug offenders and a decline in the rehabilitative ideology in the criminal justice system.[43] The historian Caroline Acker, in *Creating the American Junkie*, demonstrates that drug policy in the United States throughout the twentieth and into the twenty-first century has been, in part, the story of how persistent drug use has come to be seen as addiction, and how addiction has come to be viewed as a "profound, irredeemable deviance" best managed through punishment. Prior to the Progressive Era in the United States, drugs were widely available, often through doctors. Middle-class women, for example, were the predominate consumers of opiates, which doctors prescribed them for a variety of ailments. As the typical opiate user changed, spreading to urban, often immigrant, working-class males, discussions of the need for drug control emerged. As Acker explains, "The perception that the newer urban male addicts were fundamentally different from individuals who had become addicted medically would come to dominate public and academic views."[44] The result of this change in the "typical" drug user led to moral reforms meant to curb drug use partly through its increasing criminalization. As "science" began to dominate discussions of persistent drug use and the American Medical Association attempted to solidify the medical profession's control of drugs, drug possession was increasingly criminalized. The culmination of concern over the "new demographic subgroup" of drug users combined with the ascendance of scientific discussions of the harms of persistent opiate use led to the 1914 Harrison Narcotic Act, the federal government's first attempt to legislatively control drug use.

The debates during the Progressive Era were largely about how to characterize persistent substance use. Was it a "vice" or a "disease"? The bifurcated response to drug use throughout the twentieth and into the twenty-first century attests to the fact that competing ideas about *what* persistent drug use means relates, in part, to *who* is using the drug. As Acker points out, the idea emerged in the Progressive Era that people who became dependent on drugs through their physician were fundamentally different from those who accessed their drugs through nonmedical means. The policy implication was that the former would get treatment for their disease while the latter would be punished for their vice. Even when the latter were described as addicts, their addiction was increasingly attributed to a defect in their personality and an inferiority in their constitution; when deemed incurable the only recourse was a law enforcement response. The resolution to this debate over the meaning of persistent drug use was (and continues to be) resolved by an uneasy alliance between the use of treatment to solve the "problem" of drug use for some addicts, and the use of punishment to solve it for others. Drug courts have emerged as a "solution" that uses of both treatment and punishment. They are predicated on the notion that some addicts, while they may be sick, need the force of the courts to become law-abiding and sober.

While the drug policy era between 1919 and the mid-1960s focused on criminalization, there was an increasing emphasis, at the federal level, on the need for an expanded drug treatment system. President Nixon highlighted the importance of treatment, reflecting prevailing ideas from the medical community that addiction was a disease. Nixon provided federal funding for treatment and the National Institute on Drug Abuse, formed during his administration, in 1973. While the funding he allocated to it evidenced Nixon's support for treatment, he also vigorously supported the criminalization of drug possession, providing funding for drug interdiction and surveillance. While drug policy differed in the 1960s and 1970s from the first half of the twentieth century because of this federal emphasis on treatment, it is important to note that the criminalization of drug use continued as well. The 1970 Comprehensive Drug Abuse and Control Act created drug categorization called "schedules" (still in existence) based on the drug's potential for abuse and dependency, and its accepted medical use. This act served as a transition between the medical and criminal justice approaches—it acknowledged medical use of drugs as valid while heightening the criminalization of other drugs, including marijuana, considered to have high potential for abuse and no acknowledged medical use. It helped to cement this distinction, still in existence, between "medicine" and "drugs."

While Nixon allocated federal funding for treatment, his budget for enforcement of drug laws increased substantially as well; he also established the Drug Enforcement Agency in 1973. Nixon's administration transitioned to a drug enforcement policy that would eventually focus on enforcement and attach strong penalties, increasingly incarceration, for possession and distribution. Emboldened by the rhetoric of Nixon's tough stance on drugs, in the 1970s states began implementing highly punitive approaches to drug use that would become the model for the federal level. For example, in 1973 New York passed the Rockefeller Drug Laws, the harshest drug laws at the time, which called for a fifteen-year prison sentence for anyone convicted of selling two ounces or possessing four ounces of narcotics. Prior to this time, there were no minimum sentences for drug possession; for example, the penalty for possessing small amounts of marijuana could be probation for less than a year. Increasingly, minimum sentences in prison set by the government for drug possession became the norm.

The 1980s ushered in what David Musto has characterized as "the new intolerance" in drug policy.[45] While the experiments with hallucinogens and a liberalizing of attitudes toward marijuana prevailed in the decades before, Ronald Reagan ushered in the contemporary War on Drugs through decreased funding for treatment and increased funding for interdiction. The increased and widespread use of drug testing in the workplace was the result of a policy approach heavily focused on deterring drug use.[46] Middle- and upper-class addicts accessed treatment, often funded through health insurance, while poor drug users went to prison.[47] Reagan supported a series of acts in 1984, 1986, and 1988 that were the most stringent federal drug policies to date, requiring mandatory minimum penalties for drug possession and distribution. The 1986 and 1988 Anti–Drug Abuse Acts solidified this response toward criminalization and established the White House Office of National Drug Control Policy, cementing drug control as a national priority. Another result of these acts was a doubling of arrests for drug offenses.[48] An important factor underlying these trends was determinate sentencing requirements, which allowed judges little to no discretion in the sentencing process.[49]

As part of the increasing criminalization of drug use and users, people with felony drug-related convictions are routinely denied access to housing, education, and other social services even after they've served the time for the crime. As part of the 1996 Housing Opportunity Program Extension Act, anyone with a drug-related felony conviction can be denied access to public housing. Public housing authorities have the right to access the criminal records of any housing applicant. They also have the right to access the records from a drug treatment program the applicant might be attending so they can find out if the person is currently using an illegal drug. Entire families have been evicted from public housing because of one member's illegal drug use, a policy that was upheld by the U.S. Supreme Court in 2002. In 1998 the Higher Education Act was amended to deny people with drug-related felony convictions access to loans, grants, or work assistance for higher education. The first arrest leads to a one-year suspension of student loans, the second arrest, a two-year suspension, and a third arrest leads to permanent denial of any public funding for education. A similar policy applies to benefits under Temporary Assistance for

Needy Families: anyone with a violent or drug-related felony conviction is denied access to cash assistance and food stamps.

The triumph of the War on Drugs has been its infiltration into so many areas of human life. As the anthropologist William Garriott notes, "To live in the United States today is to participate, however modestly or vicariously, in the War on Drugs."[50] The connection between drugs and crime that has been made through the criminalization of drug use has become the "social fact" that proves the continued need for the War on Drugs, despite increasing worldwide skepticism of its efficacy.[51] The criminalization of drugs reflects our general cultural obsession with drug use and sobriety; the "war" to stop drug use reflects these broader ideological concerns and is motivated by ideas that have been solidified into punitive practice.

Ideas Matter

My research focuses specifically on the prevailing theories of addiction and recovery that drug court advocates draw on to argue for the expansion of court-mandated drug treatment. I also take an explicitly historical perspective, moving several centuries back into the history of discipline and punishment than is usually the case in studies of contemporary "innovations." This broad historical perspective departs from how I originally conceived of this research, but it gave me the historical depth to consider the significance of drug courts in a way that can easily be obscured by the myriad research articles testifying to the uniqueness of drug courts.[52]

Grounded in the sociology of knowledge, I have sought to answer the following questions: (1) How are the seemingly contradictory approaches to drug use—therapeutic and punitive—merged in the concept of drug courts? (2) What knowledge do drug court advocates use to reconstruct the problem of addiction and articulate a role for the courts in solving social problems? (3) What theories about addiction, treatment, and the problem-solving role of the criminal justice system do drug court advocates construct to justify and expand their institutions' scope?[53]

To date, the majority of research on drug courts has uniformly focused on their efficacy at reducing recidivism rates.[54] Most of this research employs large-scale quantitative methods to look at the effects of drug courts on recidivism rates. Recidivism is generally defined as re-offending in the two-year period after drug court graduation. A few of these studies have focused on the perspective of participants in drug courts, but the information gathered is generally designed to help improve drug court practice.[55] The overriding perspective of these studies is that drug courts are more effective than traditional sanctions and that this effectiveness can be measured. Importantly, most of these studies design proxy measures to stand in for the goals of drug courts. While drug courts are supposed to cure addiction, it is difficult, and in some cases impossible, to know if defendants who have graduated from these courts have, in fact, continued their abstinence from drugs and alcohol (one measurable definition of being "cured"). What can be known about them is whether they have been involved with criminal justice after participating in the drug court.

The major sociological works on drug courts, derived from observations in several courtrooms, focus largely on the judge's interaction with drug court defendants and help to shed light on actual courtroom practice.[56] These works provide important insights into the tensions in drug court operation and the often-conflicted role the judge plays as both therapeutic and punitive agent. Their ethnographic, micro-sociological focus also provides detailed descriptions of drug court practice and fits within a tradition, with studies of the criminal justice system, of in-depth courtroom observation. This approach provides a very precise understanding of how these courts operate. Because Nolan studied several different courts, his book emphasizes the highly personal nature of these courts in an attempt to explain the differences he found between his research sites. Because of judges' heavy involvement in defendants' lives and the wide discretion these courts afford them, their particular stamp on the court greatly affects the tenor of the proceedings. By moving beyond the courtroom to the level of the drug court field and its knowledge construction, my research provides a broader context in which these micro-sociological examinations can be placed. It provides a context for understanding how a particular judge might interpret addiction as a member of a society committed to the idea that deviance can and should be fixed.

When I began this study, I intended to spend time in a drug court, observing, over several months, the judge and clinical staff interact with defendants. As an introduction to this study, I attended the national drug court conference, hosted by the National Association of Drug Court Professionals, in May 2004. Afterward the focus of my research transformed considerably. I spent several days attending sessions, speaking with drug court staff, and talking with judges, researchers, and addiction counselors.

I was immediately struck by the overall ideology of drug courts and the ways that, despite individual court differences, there was a uniformity to the language drug court supporters used to talk about their work. The advocates of drug courts handed out bumper stickers and T-shirts that proclaimed "Drug Court Works," and they offered to train local courts on how to conduct National Drug Court Day activities and, importantly, on how to spread, as one person called it, "the gospel" of these courts. It was through attending this conference that I realized the importance that knowledge construction played in advancing therapeutic sanctions. This is not to imply that specific studies of courtroom practice are insignificant. Rather, I started to think about how my research could contribute to what we already knew about the reemergence of coerced drug treatment and the "activist courtroom."

Right before attending this annual conference, I also sat in and observed a large drug court in New York City. The contradictions that drug court ethnographers found were immediately apparent—for example, the judge was talking therapeutically about the benefits of treatment and the court's deep concern for a defendant whose arms were shackled and held behind her back by two guards. Combining my observation in a courtroom with my experience at the drug court conference compelled me to think of these courts in new, broader ways. Approaching it from this perspective allowed me to see these courts as symbols of transformations that were happening within punishment but also, importantly, outside it. It was this desire to get *outside* these courts and to understand their broader significance that led me to take a research approach rooted in the sociology of knowledge. It became clear to me that the practice and expansion of these courts relied heavily on transforming ideas and rhetoric about the proper role the court should and could take in the lives of defendants, and on transforming ideas about addiction as a disease that requires treatment to cure. I focused my research on the social construction of "enlightened coercion."[57]

Sociology of Knowledge

My methods have been informed, theoretically, by the sociology of knowledge, specifically as it has been used by sociologists to understand a range of phenomena where the construction of knowledge is of central practice, most notably in the construction of social problems. Attention to knowledge construction helps in understanding how reformers within the criminal justice system are able to harness theories outside this system, in this instance behavioral and medical, to argue for changes within the system. By focusing on knowledge construction within the criminal justice system but also, importantly, outside it, especially the rise of medicalized and therapeutic approaches to behavior change, I hope to show that the history of punishment is not necessarily a narrative of "progress," but rather should be read for the ways that punishment forms align with dominant cultural values.[58]

The sociology of knowledge approach, then, is one that can be usefully applied to understand the sources of ideas reformers leverage to advocate new punishment forms, without attempting to evaluate these forms' relative merits with respect to the punishment field as a whole. Rather, I connect these new punishment forms to the social and cultural trends that provide them with their theoretical and practical advantage. By linking transformations *within* punishment to trends *outside* punishment, I show the social and cultural underpinnings of punishment strategies. I also link punishment forms deemed "new" to ones that have preceded them to understand the historical development of punishment strategies.

By focusing on the social and cultural underpinnings of punishment, I am making a deliberate effort to reframe how we view transformations in punishment, which are most commonly presented for their policy, rather than cultural, significance. The published literature on the rise of rehabilitative sanctions and problem-solving courts treats these punishment strategies as relevant to policymakers whose main concerns are maximizing the efficiency of the criminal justice system, reducing recidivism rates, and spending the least amount of money to enact the most amount of change. Alternatively, this literature stresses the importance of the "theater of the courtroom" as the significant site for research, stressing that one cannot know the significance of these reforms unless one scrupulously studies the internal workings of the courtroom. I am interested in how dominant ideas that exist outside the institutions of punishment—which include advances in theories of addiction and the growing acceptance of state involvement in enforcing the health of the population—influence punishment, and how this environment provides leverage that policymakers interested in change on the *micro* (individual) and *meso* (institutional) levels can tap into when, in this instance, making the "case for coercion."

Ultimately, this project is about how knowledge is being used to reha-bilitate rehabilitation in ways that are consonant with dominant cultural ideologies about the values of both sobriety and coercion. The concept of rehabilitation was discredited in the latter half of the twentieth century by critics on the left and the right, both of whom agreed that it often led to un-equal sentences for the same crime and, according to many, simply didn't "work."[59] To rehabilitate rehabilitation, to present coerced treatment as a positive function of punishment, rather than its extreme misuse, advocates arm themselves with knowledge they hope can be used to sway people in-side the criminal justice system who have little faith in rehabilitation, and people outside the system whom they are hoping to sell, broadly, on the idea that the criminal justice system can serve the public good. My meth-ods, then, have been structured around reconstructing this knowledge to try to understand how it is used in the service of "enlightened coercion."

While this book is about the construction of knowledge that draws largely on science, it is also about its limits. Loopholes and gaps in the "sci-ence of addiction" allow for moral and personal considerations to guide the construction and presentation of the science. As I found during the course of my interviews, while advocates were armed with the latest sci-entific findings on addiction, many appealed to their personal experience with addiction as the source of their knowledge. Inevitably, when I asked about their experiences educating people about addiction, someone would say, "Everyone has had some experience with addiction," to argue for why coerced treatment has received strong support and a dearth of detractors. At a national drug court conference, I asked one drug court program co-ordinator responsible for linking defendants to treatment how she learned about addiction; she said, "I grew up with an alcoholic father. That's all the education I needed." Having worked in the field of drug policy for several years, I know firsthand the ideologies behind the "facts" of habitual sub-stance use. Most, if not all, of us have encountered habitual substance us-ers. It is this personal knowledge, often heavily tinged with a moral stance against drug use, that makes the "science" of addiction meaningful. Brain scans and medical diagnoses tell us little about the values of sobriety and abstinence from drugs, but they are products of these values.

Similarly, if one looks at the goals of drug courts, one can see that many of them, such as "leading healthy lives" or "giving back to the com-munity," have distinctly moral tones. These moral considerations are built into the goals of drug courts and the cues that drug court judges take from defendants to ensure that they are complying with the court's conception of treatment. As one advocate told me, sometimes adhering to the treatment program's protocol isn't enough; while the treatment program might say the defendant has met the program requirements, the judge might decide the person's attitude hasn't been sufficiently transformed and that they need to spend more time under court supervision, despite meeting all the program requirements and showing no toxicological signs of drug use. The "science" of addiction has little to tell us about why the judge would continue to supervise this person, but the "morality" of addiction does.

While I started my research focusing on how advocates incorporated the science of addiction into their writing and talking about coerced treatment, I emerge from this research understanding that another accomplishment of drug court advocates, and perhaps a key to their broad support, is that they appeal to people's personal experiences and moral sensibility. In doing so, they expertly blend scientific and personal knowledge, expanding what's considered the acceptable kind of knowledge that can be brought to bear on a complex problem that faces the criminal justice system. Drug courts offer an institutional or managerial solution to the problem of addiction within the criminal justice system. To make their case, though, they appeal also to the *societal* and *personal* problem of addiction, the faith in the values of sobriety and treatment, and the belief that the institutions of medicine and law can cure social problems. One of the main accomplishments of drug courts has been to positively link addiction, treatment, and coercion by arguing not only that coerced treatment is more effective than incarceration, but also that coerced treatment is more effective than voluntary treatment.

The sociology of knowledge, then, is interested in how subjective ideas come to be considered objective fact and how these ideas are used in everyday life. The necessary approach for this type of inquiry becomes interpretive; it focuses on how meaning is made through institutional logics viewed as social processes. It also focuses on how meaning is constrained through the exclusion of competing interpretations of social phenomena.[60] Institutions legitimate themselves through the knowledge they produce; they both interpret and reflect social reality. Language becomes the foundation on which these logics are constructed and disseminated.

With drug courts, scientific, moral, personal, legal, and other forms of knowledge are brought to bear with equal weight on defendants coerced into treatment. Medical and therapeutic knowledge is adopted in a legal setting. Scientific knowledge can be viewed as a form of social power, shaping knowledge and bolstering institutional practice.[61] Institutions are historical accomplishments, constituted by multiple social knowledges that make it possible for them to exert power. Power is exerted through practice, but also through abstract knowledge that legitimates and reinforces this practice.[62] The subjective nature of social problems, the fact that we understand them through interpretation, allows for reinterpretations that can alter the control brought to bear on them. Drug court advocates capitalize on this subjective nature, reframing drug offenders as addicts, which then subjects these addicts to new kinds of control called "treatment" while still retaining elements of earlier approaches, characterized by "punishment" and coercion.

Institutional practice changes partly through a reinterpretation of the social problems on which the institution is acting. Drug courts reframe the social problem the courts are responding to as one of the entrenched nature of the disease of addiction. The social problem is redefined as a hybrid medical and criminal one, with therapeutic and punitive institutions intervening in the service of "behavior change." Habitual substance use and the increasing reliance on incarceration for drug users is the social fact that gets reinterpreted as a particular kind of social *problem*, that of the disease of addiction that compels people toward criminal behavior as a result of and to sustain the addiction. Thus social problem construction can be viewed as a moral enterprise that justifies itself through scientific knowledge; social facts become certain social problems.[63]

Moral reform is a cultural act and reflects social and cultural values. The reform rhetoric is a social text that can be studied independently of the effects of the reform on individuals' behavior.[64] The language of social problems is presented through what people say and, importantly, in a knowledge-based society, what they write about their activities. A key way this happens is though the use of "scientific" data that turn moral perspectives into facts about the problem under consideration. Scientific knowledge, then, becomes another text to be studied. Rather than seeing science as presenting objective truth that is then subjectively interpreted, the science itself becomes an object of scrutiny as "a form of rhetoric."[65]

Scientific facts are presented in such a way to piece together a reality about a social phenomenon. This reality then often leads to regimes of control that resonate with people's understandings of the reality of the social problem these programs are meant to fix. It is important to dissect this reality and analyze it for its cultural underpinnings, to make the familiar strange. What if there is no such thing as addiction, understood as a chronic relapsing condition best treated through coerced sobriety? How are these prevailing constructions of addiction used as authoritative knowledge and stripped of their historical and ideological origins?

Claims are made through rhetorical work, and social problems are framed and reframed through ideas that appeal to both moral and rational arguments.[66] The constructions of social problems become institutional and cultural acts that can be analyzed for the ways they reflect and contribute to cultural understandings of social phenomena, recast as social problems. A large part of this analytic approach, of "situating" social problems, involves examining them historically. History, in this instance, becomes not a background to the contemporary construction of social problems but rather a mode of analysis, an integral component to meaningfully analyzing the construction of social problems. Historical insights help to create a "history of the present," serving an analytical purpose.[67] In this approach, I use history to debunk the notion of drug courts as a "progression" from earlier forms of punishment of criminals and treatment of drug users, instead drawing out their similarities with enduring preoccupations with normality, deviance, and social control. This approach is as much intellectual history as it is sociology. To understand why certain things are considered true, and why they are so readily accepted as truth, one must take the history of ideas into account. This type of analysis requires linking discourses of power back to the social processes and historical precedents that make these discourses possible in the first place.[68]

This approach is especially useful when one is articulating historically specific "discourses of discipline."[69] Punitive discourse has come to dominate society with considerable force. Scientific discourse has been marshaled in the service of discipline. *Judging Addicts* is the story of how seemingly contradictory approaches merge, and the story of the cultural basis of the support for coerced treatment. In this approach, the study of punishment is distinct from the discipline of criminal justice, the latter being seen as a pragmatic or policy-oriented approach that assumes the "problem" of crime to be a managerial one. I frame drug courts as a cultural and social practice and thus seek to understand the historical, social, and cultural significance of coerced treatment.[70]

The sociology of punishment does not seek to understand the effects of certain policies; it does not ask, "Do they work?" The narrow approach to criminal justice assumes, rather than questions, existing institutional frameworks and prevailing ideologies. Accordingly, the methodological approach it often uses assumes a "multivariate paradigm," seeking to understand the effects of certain interventions on behavior; it seeks correlation, which it then often conflates with causation.[71] Statistics and other kinds of measurement predominate in criminal justice research, creating, even as they appear to be measuring, an internal logic that assumes the problems of criminal justice are solely ones of administration, and that certain kinds of interventions can objectively "rehabilitate" offenders. It rarely questions why, how, and whom we punish in the first place. It does not take into account the transformations outside punishment that are reflected in the specific strategies it discusses in minute detail. It does not confront the "ideological contradictions" present in practices that are guided by punitive and therapeutic approaches.

The seeming "contradictory logics" of drug courts are readily apparent.[72] Drug courts diverge from the central logic of the criminal justice system by drawing on perspectives on drug use that are in contradiction with the traditional legalistic, case processing model. In doing so, drug court proponents argue for a new perspective that emphasizes the importance of treatment within the criminal justice system and coercion within drug treatment. I've paid particular attention to the knowledge produced by drug court advocates that attempts to reconcile these contradictory logics. What I have found is that drug court advocates have attempted to make the logics of coercion and treatment compatible rather than contradictory, and this book is, partly, the story of how they accomplish this by appealing to widespread beliefs about the importance of coercing normality and the value of sobriety.

Part of uncovering this logic involves analyzing the texts produced by organizations advocating particular punishment forms. And I have heeded punishment scholars' calls to approach these texts with a healthy skepticism toward the narratives of progress with which they are infused.[73] I subject the language, logic, and rhetoric of drug court advocates to sociological scrutiny to understand the significance of drug courts, independent of the assessment of their "revolutionary" nature offered by these same advocates. However, by taking a genealogical approach, by linking the ideas used to enact changes within the criminal justice system to ones outside it, I show the development of ideas about criminality and human behavior that inform criminal justice practice without proclaiming any one practice more "enlightened" or "progressive" than the other.

I do, however, in the concluding chapter, offer some ideas for what a radically different approach to drug use could look like. I am mindful of the privilege of my position as an academic studying policy. I have not been called on to solve crises within the criminal justice system or the seemingly intractable problem of addiction that has confounded criminal justice and drug treatment institutions and practitioners for decades. I have the luxury of standing outside, but I have attempted to respect the perspectives of those who are deeply entrenched within and who are dealing with a political reality and must offer policy solutions. I have also tried to show how those solutions are heavily embedded within ideological assumptions and faith in the criminal justice system's ability to do something "good."

I have, and draw on, many years' experience in HIV/AIDS and drug policy, for mayoral administrations in New York City and New Orleans, both cities considered to be plagued with drug and crime problems. I have conducted studies for the federal government on the implementation of drug policy in several urban areas characterized by high rates of illicit drug use. And I have helped contribute to, through policy-oriented publications, the "addiction as a disease" concepts that I critique here. I have been inside the policymaking process, concerned with programmatic outcomes and "lesser of two evils" approaches, but here I stand back and consider why the two evils—both reliant on criminal justice force and an unwavering commitment to sobriety—are so close together.

Ultimately, my aim with this exploration of the construction of "enlightened coercion" is to make contributions that extend beyond intellectual objectives. The sociologist Joseph Gusfield wrote, "To find alternative ways of seeing phenomena is to imagine that things can be otherwise."[74] With respect to drug policy, we have stopped imagining that things could be radically different. When coerced drug treatment is the only alternative to incarceration, perhaps it's time to consider an alternative way of viewing the problem. Perhaps it's time to reframe the problem that we are trying to solve.

2

Criminalizing Deviance

Reconciling the Punitive and Rehabilitative

It seems to be the fate of each generation to try and reform the inherited system of criminal justice and incarceration, and ours is no exception. This is not an uplifting history to trace but it does demonstrate the need for continuing engagement with these ever so difficult issues.
—David Rothman, *Conscience and Convenience*

THE REEMERGENCE OF rehabilitative sanctions within the criminal justice system is part of a broader process of transformation in punishment ideologies and practices. Punishment in the United States has been motivated by two main perspectives about the causes of crime. The first, often called the "classical perspective," is that crime is motivated by free will. According to this perspective, punishment should serve as a deterrent. The second view is that crime is caused by an underlying factor, such as the environment or psychological makeup of the rulebreaker. While these two perspectives seem conceptually different, throughout the history of punishment they have been combined into a hybrid system where people are held accountable for their rulebreaking while they are simultaneously punished with an array of transformative strategies meant to alter the causes of their deviance.

Cycles of Reform

The historian David Rothman has described the history of punishment in the United States as a cycle of "conscience and convenience."[1] Punishment reforms are often initiated by people interested in crafting a more humane, enlightened, and effective approach than that of the previous generation. In the course of implementation, these reforms become subject

to administrative routines and efficiency leading, often, to worse consequences than the problems the reforms intended to fix. Further, reformers
are often blinded to the possible deleterious effects of their reforms, seeing
them only in the light of "benevolence" and progress. This cycle of conscience and convenience—the well-intended motivations that propelled
the reform and the administrative convenience that causes the reform's
routinization (and sometimes perversion)—leads to a continuous cycle of
reform and institutionalization. This cycle should be understood, then, not
as progress toward a more humane approach to punishment but as a con-
tinual effort to remake and redo punishment in ways that reflect prevailing
social and cultural understandings about human nature and the causes of
and ways to control deviance.

Transformations in punishment reflect emerging ideas about human
behavior and its motivation. These ideas were initially religious in nature
and were reframed in the late nineteenth century in scientific and medical
terms. Overall, they reflect the enduring preoccupation with defining and
controlling deviance in ways that fix the nature of deviants into knowable
categories. Religious conceptions of deviance set the stage for scientific
ones; the emphasis on scientific approaches to punishment that emerged
in the Progressive Era bear a striking resemblance to, and serve as a secu-
lar extension of, religious concerns that dominated punishment during the
formation of the modern state (where such concerns about the discipline
and moral regulation of the individual and social body originated).[2]

The increasing application of punishment strategies rooted in the social, behavioral, and medical sciences has led to a defining feature of the
modern punishment system, namely, the increased rationalization of the
system of punishment along with specialization associated with different
categories of deviance. Deviants are now categorized into ever-increasing
types and managed by an increasing array of "specialists," with expertise
particular to the type of deviance over which they lay claim. Expert knowledge is thus brought to bear in helping to reorient notions of the origins
of deviance and in reframing whose jurisdiction should be responsible for
addressing and curing this deviance.

Each generation's reform efforts—in response to the previous generation's—serve not to decrease punitive control over deviance but rather
to enhance the system of control. Thus the history of punishment in the
United States is the story of the dramatic rise in the number of people incarcerated as well as the dramatic rise in the number of people supervised

under some form of "alternative" to incarceration—resulting in an expanded, rather than reduced, criminal justice system. Understanding reforms as complements to rather than replacements for previous eras' approaches helps explain the simultaneous existence of punitive and rehabilitative approaches. It also helps to understand how a system of punishment that relies on an increasing categorization of deviants into different types can exist along with a system of mass incarceration that makes little distinction among inmates. Diffuse and concentrated forms of punishment that are both normative and coercive coexist, and a tracing of punishment's history shows how these different forms have become complementary, rather than opposing, strategies for increasing the control of the criminal justice system over individuals' lives.[3]

Birth of the Prison

Punishment forms are built on assumptions about the causes of crime, and they often move back and forth between the two dominant approaches described in the introduction. Prison is seemingly one of the clearest manifestations of the idea that crime is the product of free will and that punishment should serve as a sufficient deterrent. While much contemporary writing on the criminal justice system today focuses on the prison as an institution of human warehousing and little else, its origins emerged out of religious concerns about humanity's soul and a firm belief, on the part of the institution's advocates, that prison represented a *progressive* step forward in the *humane* treatment of rulebreakers. As Rothman explained, "Prison rescued punishment, replacing a whole series of penalties that had lost usefulness and legitimacy."[4] Public displays of punishment, including hanging, torture, branding, whipping, and public shaming, reached a "crisis of legitimacy" and started to be seen as "disorderly and dangerous, garish and cruel," rather than as effective deterrents to crime whose public nature bound the community together. A "new sensibility" emerged during the Jacksonian Era in the United States about the sanctity of the body. Torture was discredited; it was not consonant with developing ideas about humane punishment. Public displays of punishment were considered demoralizing and ineffective. As Rothman points out, "The history of punishment is inseparable from the history of culture."[5] New cultural sensibilities about the sanctity of the body were both affected by but also influenced punishment strategies, viewed not as technical solutions to the problems of deviance but as reflections of dominant cultural attitudes about deviance, its origins, and its solutions.

An important part of this new sensibility was the idea that punishment should take place in enclosures; confinement emerged as the prevailing mode of humane punishment. As Rothman explains, "The permeability of eighteenth-century institutions gave way to sealed-off space."[6] Prison would transform the criminal's character; it would promote behavioral conformity as well as the personality transformation necessary to turn deviants into law-abiding members of the community. The regimented and uniform nature of prison would serve to both cure and discipline deviants while preventing future crime.

Advocates for prison developed two major theories about crime and how it could be cured or managed. Quakers believed that private prison cells would provide criminals with the solitary confinement necessary for them to contemplate their misdeeds and redirect their lives. Criminals would spend time alone and reemerge transformed because of their inward reflections. This approach characterized the first major prison in the United States, Eastern State Penitentiary in Philadelphia.

The second major idea was that inner transformation was less important than outward transformation. This led to a vastly different model of prison, characterized by Auburn Correctional Facility's focus on group behavior. Inmates were not left alone in their cells but, rather, were engaged in congregate activities where they learned to be "obedient citizens," with discipline as the guiding principle. This model assumed that people were permanently deviant and couldn't be fixed; the strategy was to tame their instincts and render them docile. The Auburn model of prison eventually prevailed, revealing the entrenched nature of Puritan ideas about deviance as manageable but never curable. While people debated the relative merits of each approach, few argued against prison, and institutions more generally, as the best places to transform deviants.

In *Wayward Puritans*, Kai Erikson expertly shows the enduring legacy of the Puritan constructions of deviance out of which prisons emerged. Puritans used deviance to help to define the "outer edges" of their society. As Erikson observes, crime is not an unfortunate by-product of society but rather an essential aspect of its formation and maintenance. Puritans accomplished this boundary-making function through a contradictory process where deviants were locked into permanent roles as rulebreakers, their depravity seen as a reflection of who they *really* were, and yet they were subject to the available treatment, as if they could be reformed. Deviants were not necessarily deserving of sympathy but were nonetheless subject to interventions at the community's disposal as part of the civilizing process, regardless of whether the deviant wanted these interventions. Puritans constructed a permanent class of deviants by defining rulebreakers as such, even if their criminal act was an aberration or a passing episode.

Because Puritans developed a strongly formed deviant identity, finding a cure was virtually impossible and yet the faith in treatment remained strong. By ascribing a permanence to a deviant's character but attempting to fix them nonetheless, the tension between determinism and free will was, and continues to be, clearly played out, with both perspectives prevailing. As Erikson explains, "The common feeling that deviant persons can never really change . . . is expressed so frequently and with such conviction that it eventually creates the facts which later 'prove' it to be correct."[7]

A clear contradiction emerges where resources are deployed to fix the deviant even in the face of the overriding and entrenched conviction that the deviant will never fully be cured. This leads to an inevitable cycle in punishment; ultimately no reform will work if the underlying premise is that deviants cannot be fixed. And yet we persist as if people can be fixed, and it's the job of reformers to develop the right strategy to cure rulebreakers. Punishment strategies, such as the Auburn model, developed to intervene at the level of behavior—encouraging the deviant to suppress their criminality precisely because they can never fully be inwardly transformed. The goal, then, is to discipline and monitor the deviant who is, by definition, incurable.

This preoccupation with managing deviance, Erikson argues, has become a permanent feature of society deeply steeped in theories of deviance's incurability. Once someone is labeled deviant, they are permanently stigmatized as such.[8] This contradiction helps to explain the persistent cycles of "conscience and convenience" that have characterized efforts to reform deviants in the United States as well as the failures of these reforms. As Rothman points out, the function of Jacksonian era punishment was to "bind together a fragmented society" in the face of a perceived increase in the disintegration of traditional social bonds (e.g., church, community, and family).[9] Punishment reflects these social anxieties, and while reformers express concern with the transformation of the deviant, they are also implicitly trying to instill social order in the face of changes that many believe would threaten social cohesion.

Progressive Era Reforms

As part of the cycle of punishment reform, prisons, once considered a progressive approach to punishment, came to be viewed as an inflexible and ineffective way to deal with rulebreakers; further, they were seen as a "shame" and a "embarrassment" because of their ineffectiveness at deterring crime and their lax, brutal, and corrupt management. Inmates were treated with indifference at best and often abused. As Rothman explains, "The well-ordered asylum had become the madhouse"; public reports of the degrading state of life in prison became widespread.[10] The Progressive Era in the United States, roughly between 1880 and 1920, marked both a shift in terms of how social problems were conceptualized and the formation of the proper solutions to these newly formulated problems. Punishment in the Progressive Era was characterized by a turn away from the exclusive use of one punishment strategy—prison—and toward efforts to identify multiple types of criminals and, accordingly, multiple types of solutions to these problems in the form of an increasing array of punishment modes. It was also a time when the use of "expertise" was rising and the burgeoning social, psychological, and medical sciences were being employed to help explain and cure deviance.

Progressive Era reformers were directly responding to what they viewed as the inflexibility of the prison system, its deleterious effects on people imprisoned, and its assumption that crime was uniformly a response to social disorder. Armed with new sociological and scientific theories about the causes of crime, they initiated reforms meant to address what had become the status quo in punishment—that is, prison (itself considered radical reform decades earlier). Arguing for individualized rehabilitation rather than uniform punishment, progressives initiated a host of reforms meant to provide the emerging punishment professionals significant discretion. Prison homogenized; Progressive Era reformers called for differentiation. Progressive Era reformers used multiple explanations for deviance, all of which posited some underlying cause for rulebreaking but tried to differentiate among different types of explanations. Some focused on the criminogenic quality of cities, arguing for environmental interpretations of the causes of deviance, while others sought medical and psychological explanations for bad behavior. Progressive Era, middle-class reformers were also active in transforming what was considered bad behavior; they increasingly defined a host of behaviors associated with urban-dwelling immigrants as unacceptable and classified these behaviors as criminal.

While Progressive Era reformers were strongly opposed to prison as the sole institution enacting punishment, they did not seek to deinstitutionalize punishment but, rather, to impose a large measure of *discretion* in the punishment system. This discretion was meant to serve as a counterbalance to the rigid administration of prison and its uniform use for criminals of all types. Rather than lessening the use of prison or the criminal justice system's hold on deviants, Progressive Era reforms added to the existing system. These reforms became "supplements to incarceration" rather than substitutes for institutionalization, and helped expand the number of people under some form of punitive oversight.[11]

One of the main ways progressives reoriented (partially) the problem of deviance toward determinist explanations and away from explicitly religious ones was by drawing on scientific theories that attempted to explain the motivation for behavior and ways to change this motivation. To accomplish the broader social transformations Progressive Era reformers were seeking, courts borrowed from disciplinary perspectives outside the realm of law. The social sciences and the medical field played a pivotal role in shaping the nature of this era's reforms. While reformers appealed to psychology, social work, and medicine, they encouraged the control of this deviant behavior to remain in the burgeoning criminal justice system.

Progressive Era Courts

Deviance was redefined with scientific explanations; these new theories about criminality were enacted through the developing court system. Progressive reformers encouraged judges to think about the environment and other social factors and to incorporate psychological and medical knowledge into their legal approach.[12] These ideas were used to justify the expansion of the state through the courts, which became an important vehicle for regulating the conduct of the population. The historian Michael Willrich has dubbed this trend "sociological jurisprudence" precisely because the new Progressive Era courts represented a rejection of the classical approach where individuals were treated as rational actors; instead, these courts attempted to intervene in the social problems these reformers believed caused criminality.[13]

These new courts embodied significant emerging trends in punishment. They were an institutionalized response to punishment that was, simultaneously, based on individualized approaches to deviance. They were an attempt to rationalize and systematize punishment based on theories about the importance of discretion. These theories of discretion were informed by behavioral and social sciences that reflected systematic approaches to understanding the relationship of the individual to their environment.

By broadening their focus, these emerging courts were able to harness considerable amounts of disciplinary power; social work, psychology, medicine, and psychiatry became integral to, and enhanced the power of, judicial practice. Courts were "rationalized" based on the new reformist theories about the role that jurisprudence could play in enacting social change, and outside "disciplinary personnel" were brought in to help enact these theories. Psychologists, psychiatrists, and social workers were the "social experts" helping the judge to understand the various forms of treatment that were available to reform offenders. At the same time, with this alliance with the criminal justice system, the modes of treatment were multiplying as were the number of "social experts" who used this newly found alliance to enhance their knowledge and expertise.

The courts were arming themselves with scientific and medicalized theories to help understand deviance and alter individual deviants. Importantly, in the process of articulating a new role for courts, these courts were also contributing to ideas about what it meant to be a "normal," law-abiding person. Intimate details of people's lives were considered the courts' jurisdiction because they were central to citizens' rulebreaking and key to figuring out how to intervene in their deviance. Thus these courts consumed knowledge but also produced it, and did so in ways that reflected the need not only to understand deviance but to govern and control it.

Juvenile Courts

Progressive Era transformations in punishment can be understood as both institutional and ideological triumphs. The development of the juvenile justice system in many ways most closely resembles drug courts, in part because of the ideological shift they represented in terms of how the emerging social disciplines were starting to differentiate among certain types of criminals, based on characteristics meant to separate them from rational adults culpable for their actions. Juvenile courts developed as a separate system of punishment for young people based on the idea that children were different than adults, could not be held responsible for their actions, and required the state's help to be rehabilitated.[14] These courts were based on the notion of *parens patriae*; the state would act as surrogate parents to the children who committed crimes, providing them with interventions developed by "scientific social work" intended to change delinquents into law-abiding adults.[15] The sociologist Barry Feld explains that these courts reflected ideological transformations crystallized in the "invention" of the category of child. The concept of "childhood" as distinct from adulthood emerged; young people were reconfigured as vulnerable, fragile, and dependent children as opposed to autonomous and responsible adults.

The *idea* of childhood, then, influenced the practices that middle-class reformers developed to deal with "other people's children"—those of immigrants—who needed sustained intervention to be inculcated into middle-class ideals.[16] Children were cast as innocent, but susceptible to corruption. Criminal involvement, the evidence for this corruption, became an opportunity to intervene in the lives of young people through a rehabilitative and therapeutic approach overseen by the juvenile justice courts. Social welfare and criminal social control were combined; individualized justice was seen as the best approach to young offenders who could be transformed through the proper application of scientific behavior change interventions and surveillance.

The juvenile justice system required the invention of childhood as the basis and justification for a separate system of justice for people defined as children. Drug courts represent a similar ideological transformation; the invention of addiction as a state marked by lack of volition and consequential thinking resembles the qualities juvenile justice reformers ascribed to children. Once the ideological and conceptual transformations are in place and widespread—*child* and *addict* as distinct from rational adult—social control practices that reflect these conceptions are the logical next step. Juvenile courts have not lessened the social control of young offenders but have altered the goals of this control. As the sociologist Mary Bortner points out in her study of juvenile courts, the notion of individual justice oriented toward social change had humanitarian roots, offering ideally "a superior justice finely tuned to restore harmony between the individual and collective."[17] The idea that individualized treatment was the best approach for juvenile offenders was motivated by "humanitarian sentiment." Bortner concludes, however, that this "powerfully seductive" ideology was "tarnished by harsh realities" where discrimination prevailed. Feld argues that these courts are based on the "conceptual flaw" that the same agency that punishes can also help, and that criminal social control and social welfare can be combined.

The contradictions in this approach are most apparent in the transformations that have taken place in juvenile justice since the mid-1970s. Increasingly, states are transferring juveniles to adult criminal court, despite what the sociologist Aaron Kupchik describes as "cultural understandings" of children not unlike those developed in the Progressive Era.[18] States are increasingly lowering the age at which young offenders can be transferred into criminal court, and creating laws, based on age or charged offense, that automatically exclude some young offenders from juvenile court. The result is a hybrid "sequential model of justice" that borrows from the criminal model—offenders should be held culpable—but also a juvenile justice model; once in criminal court, the idea that young people have reduced culpability plays a role in their prosecution as adults.

The similarities with addicts are also apparent in this sequential model. Drug courts are a hybrid criminal and therapeutic court. Addicts are mandated to rehabilitation based on the idea that they are sick with an addiction that is, in large part, the cause of their criminal behavior. And yet, if they repeatedly fail to be transformed by the court-mandated treatment, they are then processed as rational, culpable adults and sentenced accordingly. These individualized approaches rely on distinct categories of criminal offenders that are bolstered by ideologies that explain these differences. Children and addicts are distinct groups who are not wholly responsible for their crimes. And yet the increasingly punitive approach to young offenders as well as the hybrid punitive and rehabilitative approach to drug court defendants, who will most likely end up in prison if they cannot remain sober, suggests that these ideologies are as contradictory as the practices to which we subject young and addicted offenders.

Progressive Era reforms, and juvenile courts specifically, ushered in the enduring, yet fractured, idea that individualized treatment based on the application of scientific rehabilitative principles could transform certain offenders whose criminality was ascribed to a condition that rendered their culpability partial. These ideological shifts ushered in social control practices that were hybrid punitive–therapeutic interventions overseen by the courts. As Feld observes, the social welfare function of these courts are overshadowed by their crime control function, given that these rehabilitative interventions are overseen by the criminal justice system, arguably the most powerful site for controlling deviance.

Probation and Parole

While the courts played a large role in helping to enact Progressive Era reforms, they were one of many institutional frameworks developed that vastly broadened the scope of the crime control apparatus. The courts represented a "front-end" approach to crime, setting up a diagnostic, specialized, and disciplinary framework for dealing with people as they entered the system. Progressive Era reformers also felt the need to develop "back-end" systems—ones that would extend the supervisory network over people as they left the prison or treatment systems. For that reason, a system of parole that would serve to extend the network of supervision over people deemed deviant and in need of rehabilitation developed.[19]

Parole's origins in the Progressive Era were linked to the idea that isolation had deleterious effects on prisoners, and therefore offenders needed to be reformed and monitored in the "community" after they had served their period of confinement. Parole was based on an ideology of reintegration but it also served a managerial function, helping to deal with the expanding number of people coming under criminal justice supervision. Drug courts have a similar function, offering an ideology of help and rehabilitation while also providing an alternative avenue for prisoners in an era of prison overcrowding. With parole, the result has been a system that vastly broadened the supervisory scope of the criminal justice system; it simultaneously helped to build up the institutional basis of punishment while also broadening its scope out into the "community."

The sociologist Jonathan Simon, in *Poor Discipline: Parole and Social Control of the Underclass, 1890–1990*, distinguishes between phases of parole regimes and their justifications, which is helpful for understanding the shift from the kind of "socialization of law" perspective that dominated Progressive Era reforms to the more therapeutic emphasis that has emerged over the second half of the twentieth century and that characterizes drug courts today. For Simon, the need to control labor dominated Progressive Era reforms and was an explicit part of Progressive Era justifications for the type of normalizing interventions reformers advocated. The goal was to help immigrant and other groups become part of mainstream America; the criminal justice system became a means for taming deviant tendencies that undermined the burgeoning industrial economy. Parole was a means to instill labor discipline. By the 1950s, however, declines in economic production and the absence of jobs led to new justifications for parole that were de-linked from coerced participation in the labor market and connected, instead, rhetorically to notions of "personal transformation" and rehabilitation. Simon calls this "clinical parole" because it de-emphasized labor discipline while privileging individual transformation for the sake of producing normal law-abiding citizens without linking this normality explicitly to labor market participation.

The distinction between a disciplinary regime and a clinical or therapeutic one illuminates how seemingly similar reform rhetoric has transformed over time. The need for labor discipline still preoccupies people concerned with rehabilitation. In the new configuration, though, labor market participation becomes a sign or symbol of one's rehabilitation rather than, necessarily, its goal. The goal of producing "normal citizens" looms large in the discourse of drug court reformers, with the ability to hold a steady job as one sign, among many, that one is successfully engaged in the "recovery" process.

The Progressive Era represented a crucial time for both the expansion of the criminal justice system and the incorporation into criminal justice practice of explicitly therapeutic, normalizing disciplines such as psychology, psychiatry, and social work. The Progressive Era stands, in many ways, as the precursor to the reemergence of rehabilitation that drug courts—and problem-solving courts generally—represent. Progressive Era reformers were motivated by managerial concerns—containing large groups of deviants. They were also motivated by ideological concerns—using the emerging behavioral and medical sciences to classify deviants into different types, and to enact scientifically based transformations on them to ensure normalization and discipline.

While scholars of drug courts argue that these courts differ from their Progressive Era counterparts, they nonetheless resemble these courts in important ways.[20] Judges are using drug courts to articulate the importance of the courts for solving social problems, the positive role judicial discretion can and should play in transforming criminals, and the need for medical and therapeutic theories to justify their personalized and sustained behavioral interventions.

Critiques of Discretion

As part of the general cycle of conscience and convenience, there was a shift away from the discretion that, in the Progressive Era, was viewed as an enlightened approach to understanding crime and punishment. Critique emerged from all sides about discretion, with some arguing that discretion led to unequal sentences based on factors such as race, while others argued that it led to widespread leniency in sentencing. Discretion, once heralded as the benefit of Progressive Era reforms, came to have negative associations: it allowed judges or other criminal justice personnel to bend the rules and exhibit favoritism, and it allowed for too much leeway in a system that should be more standardized.

The critiques emerged in full force during the 1960s and would be incorporated beginning in the 1970s. Two changes resulted from the critiques of discretion. First, there were widespread transformations, in the form of sentencing guidelines, that would severely restrict judicial discretion and the options available to judges. Second, and related, was a widespread discrediting of the idea of rehabilitation. This is not to say that rehabilitation was removed from the criminal justice system, but its use by judges was greatly discredited as research famously emerged showing that "nothing works."[21]

Federalization of crime policy during the 1960s helped to solidify the changes that happened at the judicial level. Previously the purview of local government, crime policy became national and beholden to political concerns to an unprecedented degree. The sociologist Katherine Beckett points out that the "problem" of crime also became publicized at the national level; subsequently, the public came to see "law and order" as a serious social issue requiring a strong response.[22] This represented an important ideological shift, where the public was more likely to support punitive approaches to crime and punishment. But, as Beckett points out, "crime-related issues . . . are socially and politically constructed."[23] The rhetoric of law and order was mobilized in the 1950s, but in the 1960s the problem of "street crime" entered national political discourse. Importantly, as Beckett points out, public concern about crime did not reflect crime's increasing prevalence; rather, it reflected the increasing attention that both political elites and the media gave to these issues.

The result of this media and political attention was an increasing "get tough" discourse about crime that was accompanied by an increasingly managerial approach to criminology.[24] Criminal justice reforms such as sentencing guidelines were "an administrative effort to professionalize law enforcement officials, impose modern management techniques on criminal justice agencies, and more generally establish the idea of a criminal justice *system*" while appeasing a public increasingly fearful of crime.[25] The courts were one site where this systematization played out.

The courts were especially vulnerable to criticism because, up until the 1970s, there were virtually no sentencing guidelines, and judges could use a considerable amount of discretion when making sentencing decisions. There were scant or inconsistent criteria among judges about how to make decisions, and little agreement about what criteria should be taken into account when making sentencing decisions. The result was great disparity and a lack of "truth in sentencing," meaning that people rarely served the time for which they were sentenced because they could be released from prison early: Two people sentenced to different time periods could end up spending the same amount of time in prison. Alternately, two people convicted of the same crime could receive vastly different sentences.

The rationale for this approach—a holdover from the Progressive Era—was that individualized considerations were the only effective way to deal with offenders. These disparities, and the discretion that caused them, were highlighted as reformers argued that no demonstrable evidence existed to prove that individualized sentences altered behavior.[26] This discretion came to be viewed as not only feckless but also dangerous and authoritarian.[27]

"Truth in sentencing" statutes, which held that "equal sentences imposed in open court had to mean the same thing for different offenders," were adopted by several states.[28] Judges disagreed, however, over what sentence any particular type of case deserved. It became clear, to the vocal opponents of discretion, that a mechanism was needed to standardize sentences. This mechanism became sentencing guidelines that attempted to limit judicial discretion by imposing "objective" standards. Fairly strict sentencing guidelines emerged, where judges had little discretion in sentencing; consequently, because of longer and mandatory prison sentences for a growing number of crimes, including drug offenses, incarceration rates steadily increased.

Decline in the Rehabilitative Ideal

A second factor that contributed to the decline of judicial discretion and increasing incarceration rates was the general discrediting of the rehabilitative ideal. Scholars concerned with understanding contemporary punishment practices have documented the steady decline and virtual eradication of the rehabilitative focus in punishment since the mid-1970s.[29] The sociologists Malcolm Feeley and Jonathan Simon have labeled this era the "new penology"; it is characterized by the emergence of new "discourses, objectives and techniques" for approaching punishment that expand the number of people under criminal justice oversight, often through therapeutic sanctions.[30] While the language of rehabilitation remains, the new penology is more about "managing costs and controlling dangerous populations rather than social or personal transformation."[31]

Feeley and Simon's argument has been pivotal in helping to establish, among many sociology of punishment scholars, a dominant way of understanding punishment since the 1970s. While contemporary punishment forms may resemble past ones, Feeley and Simon argue that their rationale has changed. While deviants are routinely categorized into myriad types, a practice that emerged in the Progressive Era, this categorization is done neither to help understand them nor to cure deviance. Rather, this categorization serves managerial and risk assessment purposes. Criminals are categorized according to the level of risk they pose to society and then punished accordingly. Again, while therapeutic sanctions might be one form of punishment, according to the new penology, these punishments are only secondarily about rehabilitation; they are primarily ways of institutionally handling different forms of deviance. As Feeley and Simon explain, "Convenience has become the primary form of conscience."[32]

The new penology holds that the substantial difference between current crime control strategies and the eras where rehabilitation was a staple of the system is that no dominant narrative exists. Instead, it's a "postmodern" system precisely because there is no overarching theory under which crime control strategies can be neatly fit. Scholars of the new penology tend to idealize the rehabilitative emphasis that existed until the

1950s, underplaying its qualities of management and social control; they also overemphasize the unity that exists in punishment where, currently, a broad array of strategies are used to control offenders, with prison being only one option, albeit the most prominent.

Contradictory overarching approaches can exist simultaneously and reflect the "twin faces of punishment," incarceration and its alternatives.[33] Rather than pointing to the absence of an overarching narrative, these dual approaches demonstrate the durability, intractability, and inventiveness of the criminal justice system. Liberal and conservative approaches coexist, harking back to the tensions that have always characterized punishment, between free will and determinism. Drug and other therapeutic courts do not necessarily herald a new approach to punishment, but rather could be viewed as a form of nostalgia, a return to state paternalism.

The question of what stage of punishment we are in bears directly on how we understand drug courts and other alternatives presented as "radical" and new. Drug courts fit within the dominant framework of what the sociologist David Garland calls "penal modernism," which is a direct outgrowth of enlightenment punishment ideologies.[34] Current punishment strategies connect directly to the Progressive Era, and these strategies can be viewed as both humane and dehumanizing, progressive and reactionary. The new penology is part of this modernity where moral reform efforts still inform punishment strategies for certain offenders. As Garland explains, "While the critique of rehabilitation may have exposed the covert moralizing of penal professionals, it has done little to interrupt the task of seeking to impress different standards of conduct on individuals."[35] We are in a moment of dual and contradictory approaches to punishment. Punitive and normalizing punishment coexist, and we can see the punitive components of these rehabilitative approaches that characterize punishment as a social practice.[36]

Drug courts combine punitive and rehabilitative approaches in one punishment form. They do not fit neatly within the bifurcated nature of punishment depicted by scholars. Drug courts do expand penal control via judicial discretion and heavy defendant monitoring, but do so in ways that explicitly draw on the language of rehabilitation.[37] Drug courts are normalizing institutions but are justified, by advocates, with respect to a therapeutic logic not traditionally associated with the criminal justice system. While drug court advocates frequently mention the cost savings associated with their activities and reduced recidivism rates, they believe that the best way to achieve these is through sustained therapeutic interventions and high levels of involvement in defendants' lives.[38] Drug courts embody elements of the new penology but differ from the dominant approaches characterized by punishment scholars with their consistent concern for rehabilitation.

Drug court activities expand the boundaries of dominant criminal justice practice by defining drug use simultaneously as a criminal, medical, and behavioral problem amenable to court-monitored therapeutic interventions and traditional criminal justice sanctions. Drug courts accomplish this by drawing on "scientific" and "medical" theories of addiction to transform commonly held notions about drug use within the criminal justice system, and to argue for the expansion of coerced drug treatment.

Rehabilitation, then, can be both transformative and punitive, and an acknowledgment of its hybrid nature helps to complicate what has been depicted as a rather simple story of a "punitive turn." Drug courts embody this tension and drug court advocates are mindful of appealing to both sides of the debate by positing a form of determinism—addiction—while arguing for the importance of sanctions that rely on a rational calculation of human behavior and motivation.

In the following chapter, I focus on how drug court advocates understand their particular reform within the broader historical context detailed in this chapter. I pay attention to the problems they believe drug courts solve, and how their perspectives are informed by theories about the causes of crime and the role of courts in solving social problems. While addiction is clearly one of the problems drug court advocate believe they're solving, most of the people I interviewed focused almost exclusively on the problems within the criminal justice system as the impetus for their reform efforts. As I show in chapter 4, addiction has been increasingly subject to medicalized theories of susceptibility and therapeutic theories of treatment. However, the limits to these perspectives have provided room for the criminal justice approach—and coercion, specifically—to serve as a complement to these growing theories that simultaneously seek to find the genetic basis for addiction while locating its cure—abstinence from drugs—in the willpower of the individual. Drug court advocates enter this cycle of reform and do so in ways that attempt to transform the court system as much as the individuals subject to criminal justice oversight.

3

"The Right Thing to Do for the Right Reasons"

The Institutional Context
for the Emergence of Drug Courts

> With drug courts, people see that we're not using leeches to cure disease;
> we're switching to antibiotics. The mainstream judicial system is still us-
> ing leeches.
> —As quoted in Fox and Wolf, "The Future of Drug Courts"

DRUG COURTS EMERGED in a context of diminished judicial discretion in sentencing and harnessed widely accepted medicalized theories
of addiction. This diminished discretion reflected the discrediting of the
rehabilitative ideal in punishment and a turn toward theories of criminality that emphasized free will over deterministic causes. Reflecting the cycle
that has taken place in punishment between these two general perspectives, drug courts emerge as an attempt to shift back from the rigidity of
sentencing guidelines to the flexibility of judicial discretion. They do this
by appealing to theories of addiction that originate outside the criminal
justice system, but which they harness to bolster criminal justice oversight
of defendants deemed addicts.

In this and chapter 5, I focus specifically on how drug court proponents make their "case for coercion." Drug court proponents are actively
involved in articulating their perspectives in two key ways. The first is an
institutional perspective, whereby advocates focus their identification of the
problem as one of the failure of the courts to address the "revolving cycle"
of drug offenders in the criminal justice system. Advocates attribute a part
of this problem to the trends, discussed in chapter 2, that have eroded the
courts' ability to act with discretion for the sake of helping offenders.

Sentencing guidelines and the rise of plea-bargaining have rendered
judges with little discretion, reducing the courts' ability to be a vehicle for

"personal transformation." Drug court advocates are trying to fix the criminal justice system in part by turning courts into "problem-solving" rather than simply punitive institutions. Accordingly, I first focus on the institutional problems advocates see themselves responding to, and also their goals for drug courts at the institutional level. Advocates spoke often of wanting to rehabilitate the courts' reputation in the eyes of the public as institutions that can be responsive rather than solely punitive; I pay attention to how they construct courts as the right vehicles for curing social ills such as addiction.

A central way these advocates reframe the institutional role for the court is by identifying the *social problem* of addiction. Thus, to accomplish their rehabilitation of the court they focus on theories of rehabilitation of individuals. To do so, they construct the problem the courts face—drug-related crime—as one of "addiction." They define addiction as a disease whose treatment is best overseen by professionals with the "moral authority" to force compliance. Judges, according to this perspective, are the only professionals who can oversee this treatment precisely because their authority stems from their ability to enact meaningful sanctions, such as periodic incarceration if defendants fail to follow treatment protocols. Thus judges have the power to enact behavioral change on an unprecedented level.

Advocates reframe addiction as a disease amenable to court-mandated treatment by focusing on the behavioral outcomes of addiction. Thus they draw on the "behavioral sciences" to justify the expansion of coerced treatment. These theories lend themselves to an important feature of drug courts, the use of "graduated sanctions," and to how advocates construct the court as the ideal place to oversee treatment precisely because the judge has the power to issue sanctions with some "teeth" to them.

Related to the development of a complex system of sanctions and rewards is the centrality the idea of "relapse" plays in drug court advocates' theories of addiction. The idea that "relapse is inevitable" leads to two main features of drug courts. First, the complex systems of sanctions and rewards are predicated on the notion that addiction is a disease characterized by relapse but whose cure can be motivated by free will—namely, the desire to avoid the negative repercussions associated with continued substance use.

The second consequence is the expansion of oversight of defendants precisely because they may appear "cured" but could relapse at any moment, especially if important aspects of their lives, such as housing and employment, aren't properly secured. What exactly constitutes a "cured" drug court participant is especially problematic in the face of theories of addiction rooted in notions of the addict's ultimate incurability. By characterizing addiction as "a chronic, relapsing condition," advocates make it extremely difficult, if not impossible, to identify the moment when the disease is cured. What emerges, then, is an ongoing discussion among advocates about what actually constitutes the goal of drug courts—goals that encompass, at the level of the individual defendant, more and more aspects of their life considered to be affected by addiction and that should be considered when weighing the person's fitness to leave court supervision.

Overall, the following three chapters examine how advocates construct a problem-solving role for the court through medical theories of addiction and therapeutic theories of behavior change. By articulating such a clear role for the court, drug court advocates are involved in a reframing of the courts in two ways. First, they are attempting to reframe the courts' function as vehicles of punishment and rehabilitation. Related, they argue that punishment and coercion through the courts actually enhance treatment's effectiveness.

By entering into discussions not only about the role of the court but also about the role of coercion in treatment, drug court proponents are reframing both how we understand the function of punishment and how we understand coercion—all in the service of advancing the idea, which has clear historical roots, that the criminal justice system can and should heal; that it can and should view crime as an opportunity to rehabilitate.

Fixing the Criminal Justice System

Drug court advocates identify the problems they are addressing as institutional, internal to the criminal justice system, but propose a solution that has consequences that reach far beyond this system. To argue for the expansion of coerced treatment, drug court advocates make the case for a reorientation in the criminal justice system, and courts specifically, in addressing the problem of addiction. Their arguments about the criminal justice system's inadequate response to the "problem" of addiction rests on arguments about institutional problems—and failures—within this system as well as broader appeals for recognition that addiction, as a disease or condition *that is treatable,* motivates much criminal behavior.

Drug court advocates identify several institutional problems that served as the impetus for this particular response to drug-related offenses and offenders. Advocates are critical of how courts have operated in the past, with their lack of concern for the individual defendant, and hope, through drug courts, to show the public that courts can be institutions responsive to the "community." Drug court advocates identify specific institutional failures yet use these arguments to craft a solution that enhances, rather than reduces or eliminates, this same institution's oversight of drug-related offenders. An examination of their arguments reveals how drug court advocates are concerned partly with addressing addiction and rehabilitating offenders, but principally with rehabilitating the criminal justice system's approach by proposing a solution that retains, and perhaps expands, that system's hold on persistent substance users.

Prominent advocates of drug courts are almost uniformly people with training in the criminal justice system or law, many of whom come from a background working with the courts. Thus these advocates did not start with the problem of addiction and arrive at coerced treatment as a solution. Rather, they began with the problem of court inefficiency or unresponsiveness. They saw that drug-related offenders made up a key part of the return population to courts and decided that the disease of addiction, not an inherent propensity for criminality, was a motivating factor for these repeat offenders. Thus they concluded that the courts should respond to this addiction in ways that reflected the emerging disease model of chronic substance use, which has gained considerable public popularity over the twentieth and twenty-first centuries.

It is noteworthy that few of the people I spoke with discussed policy shifts that had resulted in the courts being overcrowded with drug-related offenders. The influx of drug-related offenders into the court system starting in the early 1980s is not necessarily a reflection of increased "addiction" or even increased substance use but rather dramatic changes in drug policy, especially the increased criminalization of illicit drug use represented by the War on Drugs. The War on Drugs precipitated aggressive efforts to find and punish illicit drug users. Fueled by the idea that illegal drug use could be stopped, in part, by aggressive policing of drug users, the result was that far more drug users were arrested, charged, sentenced, and imprisoned for drug use. The punitive approach represented by the War on

Drugs was a reflection of the changes at the state level that called for mandatory minimum sentences for drug offenders.

Combined, these increasingly punitive approaches to illicit drugs—at the federal, state, and local level—created a climate where possession of illegal drugs was far more likely to result in a prison sentence than in previous eras, and even more likely for African Americans and Latinos than for white drug users.[1] The advocates I spoke with never mentioned this discrepancy, largely the result of aggressive policing in particular neighborhoods.[2] Despite the clear role that the War on Drugs and other punitive drug policies have played in racial discrepancies in drug arrests, convictions, and sentencing, drug court advocates rarely mention dismantling criminal justice sanctions for drug offenders. Rather, they want to change the form these sanctions take. For them, the problem was one of increasing addiction accompanied by the court's inability, because of sentencing guidelines, to intervene in meaningful ways in the lives of the drug users coming through the system.

Revolving Door Justice

Uniformly, drug court advocates in interviews and documents refer to the "revolving door nature" of justice for drug offenders as the biggest institutional failure, and the impetus for drug courts. The revolving door is directly related to addiction because, as one advocate explained, "people . . . get so drug stupid they make easy arrests and become easy arrests. . . . Unfortunately for the most part many of these people go through the system their entire lives." When I asked another advocate to talk about the numbers of people who cycle through the system, he explained:

> You don't need to be a weather man to know which way the wind blows. . . . There was this observational sense . . . certainly if you talked anecdotally . . . if you grabbed a beer with the average criminal court judge, prosecutor, or defense attorney what you were hearing over and over and over again was this sense of frustration with the revolving door nature of what they do. And so much of that was linked to drug addiction.

It was, as another advocate explained, "This very ugly cycle that just goes on and on and on," the ugly cycle being addiction. Another advocate described the situation this way:

And to see you coming through day in and day out, or every thirty days, or every year or whatever. And then see your kids as soon as they're old enough to start coming through the criminal justice system. We have people, judges, who say they've got three generations of people from one family that they've adjudicated. And so it really came from that frustration that the punishment model was not working for this population.

According to drug court advocates, several pieces of this punishment model contributed directly to the revolving door of the courtroom. The first was the general punitive approach that treats drug use solely as a criminal act rather than the symptom of an illness. As one advocate characterized the dominant approach, "We keep arresting them and imprisoning them and we don't deal with addiction. Just recycle them until the drugs kill them." As someone else explained, the criminal justice system has traditionally viewed drug possession as "a slap in our face," and the response has been to "be offended." As another person argued, "As long as we remain committed as a society to punishing addiction, we are going to be losing addicts and wasting our time and money." Taking a broader view, one advocate explained the dominant approach this way:

> We've gone through twenty-five, thirty years of increasingly punitive dialogue about criminal justice, where on the national level there was this three strikes and you're out and mandatory minimums and let's extend the death penalty to new populations, let's make sure juveniles are tried as adults. These have been some of the debates that have dominated criminal justice over the past twenty or thirty years. . . . I think there's this kind of frontier justice and gunslinger ethos that's out there in American society that will always be with us.

Advocates connect this revolving door to a punitive approach to drug use, where prison becomes the dominant way of dealing with addiction—which is, for most of the advocates I spoke with, synonymous with drug use. The general punitive ethos is manifested in concrete practices that advocates identify as part of the decline in the rehabilitative ideal in punishment that contribute to the chronic recycling of drug offenders, which they believe is the main drawback of the dominant criminal justice approach. One of these approaches is the dramatic increase in the use of incarceration as a punishment for drug-related offenders. When asked to identify the main problem drug courts were responding to, one advocate responded:

> Number one is the incarceration of addicted and mentally ill people. That is the only response to drug- and alcohol-driven crime. . . . During the eighties the crack epidemic really drove eleven million people into jail and we surpassed the million incarcerated mark in the late eighties and today we're at 2.2 million and the vast majority of those people are there because of their substance abuse, their addiction. We just don't think that's right. We just don't think that prison does anything but protect society while that individual is behind bars. A great number of those people are coming out, and they're coming out in worse shape than they were when they went in.

As another advocate argued:

> Let's quit locking up addicts. . . . Some addicts will need to be locked up, that is reality, and there are many people in recovery who will tell you that it was that prison sentence that finally got my attention. But that's very different than locking everyone up.

One advocate viewed jail as an inappropriate punishment because "it's easier to go jail. . . . I've been in many jails and I know what horrendous places they are but it's easier to go to jail and just wait out the time . . . get high in jail . . . and just resume that lifestyle." Another summed up the use of jail this way: "I think that's nationally ultimately why we got into this business in the first place. Let's quit locking up addicts. Unless they are a danger to the community, let's do everything possible we can do for them before we incarcerate them long-term."

Interestingly, some reformers argue simultaneously that not enough is being done with addicts in the criminal justice system. Greg Berman and John Feinblatt, in their book *Good Courts: The Case for Problem-Solving Justice*, explain that many drug offenders are receiving "no punishment at all . . . a free ticket out of the courthouse door."[3] Because of what they identify as a dramatic increase in caseloads, courts are pressured to process defendants quickly and accept plea-bargains rather than go to trial. People differ somewhat over what they believe has contributed to these caseloads. Berman and Feinblatt argue that it is a combination of "aggressive law enforcement strategies" and "new social problems" that have led to "thousands of new cases [being] brought into the system."[4] Others identify the "crack epidemic" as the beginning of the problem, with more individuals being arrested and processed through the criminal justice system. Because of the "need for speed," Berman and Feinblatt believe that courts are compelled to resort to a "one size fits all approach" that includes, in reality, a bifurcated response, with some people going to jail but far more receiving probation as punishment.

Drug court advocates view prison as an ineffective way to deal with addicts. In this respect, they are like their Progressive Era counterparts who came to see prison as at best ineffective, and at worst a place that permitted and even encouraged criminal behavior (here, in the form of drug use). Similar to Progressive Era reformers, too, they focus almost exclusively on punishment, viewing it as the mechanism that could transform deviant behavior, if properly applied. They assume that addiction has increased, that generations of families are addicts, and that the criminal justice system should do something about this. They argue against the dominant practice of incarceration, but not policing and other front-end practices that facilitate people's involvement with the criminal justice system in the first place.

Uniformly, advocates excoriated probation and its overall ineffectiveness. Berman and Feinblatt explain: "Probation departments in many states are the bastard stepchildren of the local criminal justice system—underfunded and largely ignored. As a result, the probation system in many parts of the country is on the brink of collapse."[5] Drug court advocates believe that probation is especially ill-suited to address the needs of addicts. As one advocate explained:

> The probation model, where the person doesn't report for weeks, has dirty urines for weeks, gets picked up on some bullshit charges and then six months later files a VOP [violation of probation] and says you've been screwing up. Well, it's like kids. You don't punish a child for something they did six months ago because it's going to have absolutely no impact at all on their behavior.

As another advocate explained, "It was just the need for somebody in the criminal justice system to respond quickly to behavior and to keep people engaged in treatment when they wanted to quit. And probation didn't have that power and . . . felony offenders knew that." So, while advocates don't believe the concentrated space of prison is the right place for most addicts, they also don't believe probation offers enough surveillance—that it is too under-resourced to effectively, meaning swiftly, punish addicts when they use drugs.

Although most advocates I spoke with presented drug courts, and coerced treatment, as a new model, I did ask them about Treatment Alternatives to Street Crime (TASC), a criminal justice strategy that links defendants to treatment. Drug court advocates critique TASC for similar reasons as probation, namely, the lack of force behind it. As one advocate explained:

> TASC . . . did not use the coercive power of the court in a direct way. . . . When a client went to TASC, I never heard of him again, the judge never heard of him again, unless and until he got kicked out of treatment and he went away for four and a half to nine years, or the rare ones succeeded and it was like congratulations, good-bye. So the court was not involved except in this abstract [way], well, abstract until you get in prison. There was no court involvement.

One advocate explained the advantage of the drug court model over TASC this way:

> The drug court model is driven by and led by judges and that is the bottom-line difference between any other initiative that has ever come down the pike. TASC got real close, but as a case management strategy it was driven by case management, with the goal of linking treatment and the judiciary. . . . But a TASC case manager can't change sentencing practice. They can't call a meeting with all the key decision makers, including the sheriff and the director of substance abuse for the county, they can't bring those key decision makers to the table and effect change. A judge can.

While advocates critique the criminal justice system's response to addiction on several levels, they are equally critical of reforms that would minimize the criminal justice system's hold on drug-related offenders. Similar to their critiques of probation and TASC, advocates believe that the coercive power of the criminal justice system can be harnessed to the benefit of addicts, and that this coercion is the key to getting people "clean and sober."

Drug court advocates had even stronger words about more recent attempts to move individuals arrested for drug-related crimes into drug treatment than they did about prison and probation. They were particularly vocal when I asked them about Proposition 36. Officially known as the Substance Abuse and Crime Prevention Act, Proposition 36, a ballot initiative, went into effect in California in July 2001. Proposition 36 stipulates that first- and second-time, non-felony offenders arrested for drug possession should be rerouted to treatment instead of jail. In effect, these offenders are taken out of the criminal justice system and placed in drug treatment, with no judicial oversight once in treatment. As one advocate explained, "Prop. 36 removes the ability to put people in jail, which most drug courts believe is key."

Drug court advocates do not view jail as a problem when it is used as a therapeutic rather than a punitive tool. Therefore, while they are opposed to incarceration as the sole strategy for punishing addicts, they do believe it has important therapeutic value. As another advocate explained, "Prop. 36 is treatment driven. . . . Proposition 36 gave up the power of the judge. . . . Basically there's no consequence to repeat drug use. . . . What's kind of nutty about Prop. 36 is that you as an addict are given all this opportunity and rope to basically hang yourself, three strikes, you're out and you're off to prison." The main problem with Proposition 36, another advocate explained, is that it tells drug users "there's basically no consequence to repeated drug use." Equating Proposition 36 with legalization of drugs, they argued, "With decriminalization . . . we lose something very valuable. . . . We lose the coercive power to get people into treatment who don't want it and to keep people there who don't want to stay there. And it's just too clear that that's really important. . . . Drug courts get as close to decriminalization without toppling over and losing that coercive power." Another advocate viewed "this movement toward this sort of Prop. 36 model is an explicit attack on drug courts."

Drug court advocates have characterized Proposition 36 and other similar state-level efforts to move drug offenders into treatment as attempts to "further the agenda of legalization." In a revealingly titled article, "Ballot Initiatives: Wolves in Sheep's Clothing," the National Association of Drug Court Professionals argued against these alternatives, explaining that "immediate accountability and a one-to-one relationship with the judge" are the "hallmarks of drug courts" that help "substance-abusing defendants become productive members of society, while public safety is dramatically increased."[6] Further, they argue that "immediate sanctions (including jail) and incentives are critical to ensuring the success of the drug court participant," and describe efforts to undermine the judge's power as "veiled attempts at legalization and the public should be alerted to the true motives of those who are backing them."[7] Ironically, although drug court advocates share a similar critique with proponents of Proposition 36–type initiatives—namely, that the overuse of incarceration for drug-related offenders is misguided and ineffective—they reassert the punitive framework for drug offenders, specifically the use of jail and other immediate sanctions, to argue for the benefits of drug court–style rehabilitation.

Drug court advocates are responding to concrete problems with the administration of the criminal justice system yet firmly believe that coercion, one of the defining aspects of this system, can be harnessed for the good of addicts and in the name of recovery. To make this argument, they center much of their specific critique of the criminal justice system on sentencing practices that have taken away judicial power, which drug court advocates believe can be mobilized in ways that acknowledge addiction and facilitate recovery. Drug court advocates speak about the punitive turn in punishment, the overuse of incarceration, the ineffectiveness of parole and other alternatives—all factors that have been used to argue for the decriminalization or legalization of drug use. However, they use these arguments to advance specific reforms that will address the loss of judicial power that resulted from transformations in sentencing practices, and the negative effect these practices have had on how the public perceives the effectiveness of courts.

Drug court advocates are, first and foremost, interested in criminal justice reform, and focus this reform on the processing of drug offenders. They are not interested in drug policy reform or alternative ways to address the needs of addicts, and they are quite vocal against options such as decriminalization or legalization. As one advocate explained:

> The legalizers have a great argument outside of drug court. Who would not agree ten years ago that the War on Drugs is failing? Drug court plopped right in the middle of that argument and said there's something in between, there's an [intermediate] step of blending treatment and the

justice system. . . . You don't have to legalize it, you don't have to put my kids in harm's way, trying something because it's so readily available. . . . I think we've made it much harder for the legalizers and the decriminalizers to say there's a pressing need to get this out of the justice system.

Logic of Caring

Drug court advocates, when talking about the institutional context for the emergence of this specific form of coerced treatment, reflect the balance between the punitive and the rehabilitative, the need to be both "tough" and "caring," that is at the root of these courts. When discussing these courts, and specifically some of the first ones, advocates explain these transformations in terms of a logic of caring that they believe has been missing. One advocate explained that drug courts were "unselfish and natural in [their] origins." Another explained, "It's very much saving souls. . . . It's total enthusiasm. All good. All people who were in this because they were really interested in helping people and they were very excited about that and that was part of their calling. . . . So there was all this real rabid excitement." According to another advocate, drug courts formed because "there were criminal justice people out there who have a heart and want to do the right thing." Drug courts are "the right thing to do for the right reasons." The right thing is showing that courts care about people, in a reversal of the trend that had relegated judges to the largely technical role of dispensing preset sentences.

As one advocate explained, "Let's face it, all the problems end up on the doorstep of the courts and the courts better start thinking about what to do about it." Again, there was no discussion of policing and other practices that made it so that the criminal justice system is dealing with so many "problems" in the first place. According to a drug court judge:

Courts didn't go out and ask for everybody to come to us for help on how to get clean and sober and how to stop committing crime, but apparently we were sitting there waiting. The court system has been increasingly called on to do a lot of the things that used to be done out in the community. As a court system, we had a choice of saying, "That's really not our responsibility; we're a court system that sits there and says, 'Granted, denied, overruled, sustained,'" or saying, "Well, we accept that challenge and we'll put something together that will help solve the problem." What the courts did, to their credit, was to embrace that responsibility.[8]

The caring that drug court advocates identify as the motivation for these courts' development was a direct outgrowth of the steady decline in judicial discretion. It is also the result of what they believe has been eroding public faith in courts as relevant institutions able to act for the social good. As one advocate explained:

> For longer than two hundred years, courts have been pretty static. . . . For a whole lot of people, courts are not relevant. I firmly believe in the rule of law, but the rule of law has got to change and it's got to . . . be relevant to everyone. . . . I think the court needs to respond and show some leadership. . . . We need courts that operate, function, are relevant to the people that they serve. . . . I think drug court can make them more relevant.

The way the courts show their relevance, according to these advocates, is, in part, by showing compassion and understanding for the problems of defendants. Drug court judges, then, "are people thinking it's really good to be in public service again, and to make a difference. It's opened the vocabulary of what it means to be a court and a judge. . . . There's some wonderful and extraordinary courts. . . . Now the idea that the courts are supposed to help them with all the problems that come to them is not so crazy." Drug court judges are "a very compassionate group and we want to help people."[9] Advocates I spoke with uniformly expressed sentiments similar to this one when describing the origins of drug courts: "It was all collegial, elbow grease, creative, innovative, only people who were really doing it because they cared."

Yet, while drug court advocates want to inject the courts with more compassion and concern, they are mindful of presenting what they're doing in ways that are sufficiently attentive to the court's punitive, as well as potentially rehabilitative, purpose. While advocates talked about the compassion and selflessness of the initial drug court staff, they were also mindful to remind me, as one advocate phrased it, that "drug courts came about out of total frustration, not out of liberal bent." As another advocate emphatically explained, "I'm not a bleeding heart liberal. . . . I'll pull the trigger for people, but I want to make sure it's the right people. And I think we can fix folks." As this same advocate explained, "I think you need to have the tough side in law enforcement and the courts need to project that. . . .

So, you've got to take care of business. But drug court is a better way of taking care of business than locking them up forever."

Advocates attribute the success of drug courts, in part, to their "bipartisan recognition that the system that had been used had manifestly failed." As one advocate explained:

> The nice thing about drug courts . . . is that it appeals to both sides of the aisle. It holds offenders accountable in ways that are often unpleasant to offenders. It holds people accountable in hopes of helping them achieve sobriety and that's hard and it's painful. It's easier to go to jail. . . . That unpleasantness appeals to certain parts of society that say these guys should be punished. And simultaneously it appeals to people that wanted to see good use of public dollars, and to contribute to law abiding and a reduction in recidivism and victimization and all those things I think many people in society view as dollars well spent. And then you've got folks who look at this as a humanitarian undertaking, who see the prime job of government to improve the human condition and that appeals to them. So, you look at that spectrum and you have this one little program and it means something so significantly different to each of those factions.

Drug courts, according to advocates, allowed courts to reorient themselves toward a more compassionate and caring approach to drug use while retaining a sufficient amount of punitiveness to appease people who believe that the criminal justice system's primary function is to punish. In doing so drug courts offer, according to another advocate, less of a bipartisan option than a "third way":

> They're a classic Clintonian third path liberalism reform movement in that there are elements of the conservative approach embedded in them. This is rehabilitation for a new generation. So, it's not a rehabilitation that's a get out of jail card or that's, we're sorry because there's root causes of crime and we're going to explain away your behavior or absolve you of your individual responsibility. It's an approach that combines punishment and health and contains elements of a classic punitive model but also a classic rehabilitative model.

This political appeal—drug courts are both tough on defendants while acknowledging they have a disease and need treatment—reflects the hold that the criminal justice perspective retains despite the proliferation of a disease model of addiction. Locating the origins of compulsive substance use in the brain is not incompatible with a punitive approach when we distinguish the illness of addiction from its symptoms, one of which is, according to drug court advocates, criminal behavior. Advocates bridge these seemingly contradictory approaches, broadly characterized as medical and punitive, by arguing that the clear threat of punishment actually enhances treatment effectiveness.

Drug courts advocates highlight institutional factors that have led to the need for a more caring criminal justice response to drug use, defined as addiction. They enter into the discussion about what causes *crime* by arguing that it is determined by the *disease* of addiction. Similar to their Progressive Era counterpart courts, they are interested in how "justice" is administered and want to see courts as therapeutic and punitive vehicles for personal transformation. They argue that it should be the courts' function to coerce behavioral transformations on a group of rulebreakers who are criminal but also sick. It is by crafting specific arguments about the nature of addiction that these advocates most clearly make their case for courts as the best place to enact these kinds of transformations. In doing so, they explicitly echo the Progressive Era arguments about the need for both prison and a diverse array of therapeutic approaches, the need for both concentrated and diffuse strategies to deal with deviance, which is framed in explicitly psychological and medical terms.

4

"Enlightened Coercion"

Making Coercion Work

The very concept of health implies a positive value that one cannot but choose.
　　　　　　　　—Richard Klein, "What Is Health and How Do You Get It?"

THE REEMERGENCE OF drug courts is largely influenced by trends that have taken place outside the realm of punishment, which affect the specific knowledge that advocates draw on to argue for the importance of enlightened coercion. Two interrelated trends have paved the way for the reemergence of rehabilitative sanctions generally, and have shaped the specific ways that knowledge about addiction has been used to reorient the courts toward a "healing" function. First, the rise of medicalized processes generally, and second, the proliferation of scientific theories about the origins of addiction, have provided the dominant ways of understanding human behavior and motivation and, importantly, how to act to change this behavior.

Medicalization of Deviance

Medical interpretations of deviant behavior have come, in the late twentieth and early twenty-first centuries, to dominate society's understanding of what causes people to break norms and how to "fix" this rulebreaking. The sociologists Peter Conrad and Joseph Schneider defined medicalization as a "type of social control that involves defining a behavior as an illness primarily because of the social and ideological benefits accrued by conceptualizing it in medical terms."[1]

Redefining social problems as medical can lead to their decriminalization. As deviance is transformed from religious to criminal to medical problems, the blame on the individual for their deviant behavior is less-ened. While medical understandings form a sort of social control, blame is removed from the deviant individual, redefined from "bad" to "sick." People are not in control of their deviance, and because of the proliferation of medical technology, they are able to control or fix their deviant behavior under the authority of medical professionals. According to medicalization scholars, medicine has become the dominant normalizing institution of society, taking over for religion and law.[2]

One effect of the medicalization process is the tendency to define more and more behaviors once considered "normal," or at least not problematic, as somehow deviant, thereby increasing the aspects of human life and be-havior that are subjected to the medical gaze and interventions.[3] Human behavior is increasingly understood in terms of health and illness. Uncer-tainty is explained by medical diagnosis, even when treatment is nebulous or nonexistent.[4] Disease categories impose order. Diagnosis becomes the key to control and cements medical logic as the explanatory factor for un-derstanding more and more aspects of human life.

Medical explanations are not just grafted onto existing deviant behavior but are used to encompass greater areas of human life into the categories of illness, disease, and deviance in the first place. As the sociologist Irving Zola explains, the increasing proliferation of medical understandings of human behavior "is largely an insidious phenomenon accomplished by 'medicalizing' much of daily living by making medicine and the labels 'healthy' and 'ill' relevant to an ever increasing part of human existence."[5] Medicalization, then, is a process and an "accomplishment."[6] While mul-tiple explanations may exist for deviant behavior, medicalized theories predominate partly because they offer a homogenizing and socially shared way of understanding aspects of human life that are considered to be out-side of one's control.[7] By moving from an identification of *disease* to a focus on *health*, the scope and reach of medicalization expands.[8]

One of the reasons that the medicalization of deviance is often pre-sented as progress is because it represents a more scientific approach to understanding the causes of, and ways to cure, aberrant behavior. Medi-cal understandings are presented as value-neutral, but in fact these under-standings are deeply moral in nature. Medicalization, as a moral enterprise, is both an institutional and a cultural accomplishment.[9] It affects how we understand what it means to be human; it constitutes selves even as it pur-ports to describe them.[10] The concepts "normal" and "healthy" then are not just descriptors but rather serve to create ideals to which we should strive.[11] Health statistics provide us with a guide to what we should strive for, serving to orient our actions toward a generalized concept of good health and constituting us as people who *should* want to be healthy. Thus medicalization refers to both the institutional setting where deviance is controlled (e.g., hospitals, doctors' offices, drug treatment programs) and a cultural adoption of the frames of disease, health, and illness that affect life outside these institutional settings. Drug courts, for example, are a reflection of the culture's adoption of medical understandings of deviance as much as they are institutional ways of managing criminal bodies.

Medicalization—and the notions of health and illness—are *scientific* ways to help us understand human behavior that reflect the prevailing *social* order.[12] They produce scientific certainty among cultural uncertainty. This uncertainty is, in part, reflected in aspects of human life that are not subjected solely to the medical gaze, the understanding of which are, at best, partially subject to the logic of disease and the physician's scrutiny.

Despite this emphasis on medicalization as a dominant process in society, medicalized interpretations in fact have only a partial, and certainly incomplete, hold. Medical ideology prevails even when medicine has little to offer or collaborates with other institutions to make its force more effectively felt. It is through this "medical collaboration" that increasingly more people are brought under the category of disease and sickness.[13] Some conditions, such as addiction, are often explained with respect to medical ideology but may have little or no medical technology or medical personnel overseeing the condition's treatment. In fact, the treatment may involve no medical intervention despite the disease designation.

This gray area—where medicalized interpretations meet non-medical institutional settings—provides an important opportunity to understand the limits of the medicalization process, despite its powerful hold on contemporary society. The sociologist Peter Conrad has identified three levels of medicalization: conceptual, institutional, and interactional. Conceptual medicalization involves defining a problem in medical terms but does not require a physician to be involved in diagnosis or treatment. At this stage the language of disease is used—people are called "sick"—but the treatment is divorced from the professional and institutional settings of medicine. With the second level—"institutional medicalization"—organizations adopt a medical approach to the problems they deal with, and physicians may be involved as legitimating experts but not directly in diagnosis and treatment. "Interactional medicalization" occurs through the doctor–patient interaction, whereby a physician defines a problem as medical and treats it directly with a medical form of treatment.[14]

These levels help to understand and to distinguish different ways in which medical ideology may proliferate institutionally and culturally. Addiction provides an important arena for understanding the limits to the medical model. Theories of addiction—and drug use more generally—are an important example of how medicalized and criminalized perspectives of behavior exist simultaneously and can serve to reinforce, rather than negate or undermine, each other.

Although drug court judges often refer to addiction as a "biopsychosocial disease," physicians are rarely involved in drug court operation.[15] Drug court judges or other staff, not physicians, diagnose defendants as addicts, and drug court staff prescribe the course of treatment. In the majority of drug courts, judges can override the clinical recommendations of treatment programs.[16] While drug court judges draw parallels between addiction and chronic diseases such as diabetes, drug court defendants are punished for exhibiting the symptom of their disease—drug use—in ways that are not common with other noncontagious conditions. Drug court advocates claim they turned to the "medical community" to understand addiction, yet medical practitioners remain at the periphery of drug court practice—for example, no medical professionals are on the board of the National Association of Drug Court Professionals. Drug courts appeal to cultural understandings that are bolstered by the "science of addiction" as well as people's lay understanding of habitual substance use as a compulsive and undesirable behavior.

The cultural proliferation of the concepts of health and illness and their expanding social reach can be tied to the simultaneous intensification of medicalization, reconfigured as *biomedicalization*.[17] While medical explanations are technologically oriented, relying on increasingly specialized methods and interventions, more people are reconstituted through these explanations that encompass within them a responsibility toward health at the population level. Risk and surveillance have become key concepts that expand the medical gaze; they create disciplined bodies, ever vigilant about their health because they are potentially always at risk of disease. Health, in the era of biomedicine, is a "matter of ongoing moral self-transformation."[18] Biomedicalization is a process, then, that relies on both specialized medical expertise for its articulation while it "travels widely," creating a population increasingly oriented toward thinking in terms of health and subject to customized interventions meant to address each person's specific risk factors. In the era of biomedicalization, addiction becomes an almost ideal example of these processes. Addiction is a knowledge system that is predicated on the notion of the normal, sober body that is both an ideal, difficult to achieve, but also one people should strive to achieve through control. Addiction's flexibility as a biomedical category is evidenced by the fact that it is characterized both as a disease, cured through individually tailored treatment, and a moral failing, punished through a variety of coercive sanctions.

Medicalization of Addiction

Addiction serves as an important area to study the intersection of the punitive and medical because of the fact that it has been, and continues to be, contested terrain. The recent trend among researchers has been to increasingly define addiction not only as a disease but as a disease of the *brain*, a neurological disorder. The National Institute on Drug Abuse, the most prominent organization in the United States devoted to the scientific study of addiction, explains, in a report titled "Drugs, Brains and Behavior: The Science of Addiction," that "addiction is . . . a chronic, relapsing brain disease. . . . It is characterized as a brain disease because drugs change the brain—they change its structure and how it works."[19] The contemporary emphasis in research on addiction has been to identify not only areas of the brain *affected* by drugs but to develop theories of addiction's *origins* in the brain. Accordingly, NIDA's research efforts are now directed toward the "search for the genetic variations that contribute to the development and progression of the disease."[20] However, the historical work on theories of addiction, and the rise of notions of compulsivity with respect to drugs in the first place, show that this has been a consistent preoccupation that predates, and has developed alongside, the development of the medical profession. It also shows that transforming compulsive substance use into a deviant state has been a preoccupation of middle-class reformers interested in containing and controlling the behavior of immigrant groups, whose values were seen as a potential threat to the developing social order in the United States as industrialization was taking hold.

Understanding the social uses of theories of substance use and addiction is a key to elucidating the scientific "discoveries" used to bolster these theories and the policy implications to which they give rise. The sociologist Craig Reinarman reminds us that the ubiquity of the disease model of addiction is a "social accomplishment," the result of historical and cultural actions and discursive practices.[21] A critical examination of historical transformations in theories of habitual substance use reveals the way that the "facts" of addiction have been constructed.

The effort to define habitual substance use as the disease of addiction began in the same era that many of the "modern" approaches to punishment, detailed in chapter 2, were developed. In fact, they emerged out of similar historical conditions, namely, the need to impose order on a burgeoning society in the United States. The sociologist Harry Levine located the emergence of a disease model of addiction in the late eighteenth century, when people started viewing habitual substance use as a problem outside the individual's control.[22] While conceptions of disease when applied to substance use have changed over time, that people attempt to understand substance use as a disease (however constructed) has been consistent since the early nineteenth century in the United States. During this time, notions of how to understand "habitual drunkenness" underwent key shifts. According to Levine, during the seventeenth and eighteenth centuries the assumption was that people got drunk because they wanted to or because they loved to drink. While "habitual drunkards" were often considered a nuisance, their relationship to alcohol was not described in pejorative or, importantly, *compulsive* terms. Habitual drunkards drank because they liked to, not because they were unable to control themselves. As Levine explains, in the early nineteenth century new theories of addiction emerged, guided largely by temperance advocates, many of whom were physicians, who reoriented concepts of habitual drunkenness, and laypeople who were ready to attest to the veracity of these new theories. This transformation in how people understood habitual substance use, this "discovery of addiction," was a reflection of transformations in social life and the structure of society.

Addiction's origins were located in the individual body, the inability of the "habitual drunkard" to stop drinking alcohol, and the emerging idea that such individuals derived no pleasure from alcohol consumption. Temperance advocates reframed habitual drunkards as out of control: these individuals wanted to stop drinking but could not; therefore they did not enjoy drinking and derived no pleasure from inebriation. Words such as "overwhelming" and "overpowering" emerged to describe the drunkard's relationship to alcohol. Abstinence was seen as the only cure for habitual drunkenness, which came to be viewed as a disease. Explanations about habitual drunkenness and efforts to get drunkards to stop drinking focused on the individual's "will." According to Levine, alcoholism came to be viewed as "as a sort of disease of the will, an inability to prevent oneself from drinking."[23] Importantly, this notion of "will" persists in contemporary theories of addiction despite the increasing attempts to explain and locate the origins of compulsivity or addiction in the individual's brain.[24] Despite advances in the "evidence" that addiction is a disease, the vast majority of interventions to treat this disease rely largely on the addict's will to stop as the primary motivation for "curing" the disease.[25]

Colonial conceptions of alcohol consumption as normal, even if some viewed it as a sin, were replaced by the "discovery" of addiction by physicians who attempted to distinguish desire from will, pleasure from loss of control. This discovery, led largely by the physician Benjamin Rush, contributed four key ideas about addiction that have held sway, to varying degrees, even as theories of addiction have transformed since the late nineteenth century: first, that there is a causal agent for addiction—alcohol or "spirituous liquors"; second, that addiction constitutes a loss of control over this causal agent, a form of compulsivity; third, that this condition is in fact a disease; and, fourth, that total abstinence from the casual agent is the only way to cure the disease. Compulsion was the disease, loss of control and inebriation the symptoms, and abstinence the cure. Temperance advocates linked drunkenness to a whole host of social ills—disease, poverty and, importantly, crime—in their attempts to achieve large-scale social reform.

Transforming notions of addiction accompanied a new emphasis on the individual. While Prohibition advocates focused on the scourge of alcohol, attempting to control and eliminate its consumption by prohibiting its production and distribution, advocates of the disease model of addiction focused their efforts on the individual. It was largely the failure of the Prohibition movement that opened the door to new ways of thinking about addiction. It was in this vacuum that theories of addiction, rooted in the individual, emerged; these theories attempted to explain why some people became addicted to substances that others could consume noncompulsively. The "inner experience of the alcoholic" became a focus of people interested in addiction, and from this focus a highly individualized perspective on addiction took root.

This individualism has been a key to understanding addiction and drug use for much of the twentieth and into the twenty-first century, whether the approach has been one of medicalization, criminalization, or a combination of these two approaches. The ideas underpinning the temperance movement were directly related to Jacksonian ideas that led to the formation of the penitentiary. Both were concerned with helping people gain control over behavior considered damaging to themselves and society. The reforms that were implemented could take both assimilative and coercive forms, depending on how the designated deviant responded to the efforts of reformers.[26]

This distinction between assimilative and coercive reform, first articulated by Joseph Gusfield in *Symbolic Crusade: Status Politics and the American Temperance Movement*, continues to play an important role in understanding how normalizing discourses are acted out by the people who are the focus of this normalization, as well as what happens when individuals refuse to adhere to norms of behavior established by reformers. Assimilative reform seeks to integrate the repentant deviant back into the social order, even if tenuously. This conditional reintegration is dependent on the deviant's expressed belief in the dominant ideology about his or her transgressions; he or she must want to be fixed according to prevailing norms but needs help doing so. Thus assimilative reform is characterized by sympathy for the transgressor, viewed as morally inferior but capable of a partial recovery to the dominant norm.

With assimilative reform, the dominant mode of persuading people to adhere to norms is social programs that attempt to help the deviant behave in accordance with the values of the majority. The difficulty for the reformer arises, however, when the deviant no longer adheres to the reformer's values. These "enemies" do not respect the norms of the dominant society and cannot be made, through compassionate persuasion, to adopt these norms. Rather, the need for coercive reforms is required to alter the behavior of those who are hostile to the values of the reformer. Drug courts represent a hybrid of this approach. They are both assimilative and coercive; defendants are both repentant and guilty.

In reality, assimilative and coercive modes of reform have existed side by side and are often reflected in any given approach to the problem of substance use and addiction. These approaches are informed by theories about the alterability of human behavior sometimes taking into account speculation about the deviant's desire to have her or his behavior altered. When applied to the history of addiction, and substance use generally, it is clear that many strategies are both assimilative and coercive and are motivated by punitive and therapeutic approaches to substance use. Drug courts serve as the perfect example of these hybrid approaches. Drug courts rely heavily on the idea that addicts want to change but, because of their disease, are unable to; coercion is necessary to facilitate recovery. Defendants offered the option of drug court are able to "choose" to attend treatment over prison, and by choosing treatment they are, theoretically, ascribing to the dominant norms of sobriety: abstinence from drugs, and the notion that their criminal behavior is motivated by a compulsive addiction beyond their control.

That assimilation and coercion can coexist in one approach speaks directly to the limits of the medical model, particularly as it applies to addiction. Proponents of the disease model must engage in "conceptual acrobatics" to use the disease framework to justify seemingly contradictory approaches such as treatment on the one hand, and punishment on the other.[27] Despite the fact that the disease model produces very different responses to, and ways of treating, addiction, it is so widespread that it is difficult, if not impossible, to imagine alternate ways of thinking about drugs and drug users.

If we consider the disease concept of addiction as a process rather than a fact, a historical and discursive accomplishment rather than a scientific discovery, we can see how the myriad responses to this disease conceptualization not only reflect prevailing notions of addiction but also contribute to these very notions. Drug court proponents not only harness existing theories of addiction to justify coerced treatment but, by coercing treatment, contribute their own theories about the role that coercion *should* play in helping to cure addicts.

More recent conceptions of addiction, stemming from the processes of biomedicalization, are attempting to advance science's hold on addiction, locating it not in a diseased body but in a disordered brain.[28] The "neurobiological addict" has emerged out of these attempts to locate the disease of addiction in the brain; the addict's "neurobiological constitution" has become the site of intervention.[29] In this newly emerging framework for thinking about addiction, neuroscience focuses on "craving" and "relapse" as biologically constituted processes rather than the behavioral aspects of addiction that have proved so troublesome for a sobriety-focused society.[30] Technologies such as anti-craving medications intervene, treating a disease framed by neuroscience in terms of a disturbed reward-and-pleasure system, where the primitive part of the brain has taken over the higher, civilized part in a reversal of how things "should" be.[31] The "hijacked brain" depicted in HBO's *Addiction* series is no longer reasonable and rational, with most activities oriented toward "drug seeking." The sociologist Scott Vrecko argues that we should view anti-craving and other technoscientific addiction interventions as "civilizing technologies" rather than treatment. The civilized brain is restored through these interventions; we know they "work" when the addict's behavior begins to resemble socially constituted ideas about how people should be; "treatment" is a mechanism for regulation back to civilized conduct.

While scholars have identified and stressed the significance of neuroscientific constructions of addiction, the limitations of this perspective are broadly apparent. If we focus on these emerging biomedical constructions and the interventions that stem from them, we ignore the fact that these interventions are used for the minority of people identified as addicts. In the end, problematic substance users are identified through their behavior; we don't (yet!) scan people's brains, identify their addiction, and coerce them into drug treatment. What addiction is, what it means, and how it should be managed are contested despite the invention of drugs to cure craving or replacement therapies meant to divert substance users from illegal substances ("drugs") to legal substances ("medicine"). As Helen Keane and Kelly Hamill explain, "A recalcitrant contestability and instability . . . haunt the science of desire, compulsion and excess."[32] Addiction is a "hybrid entity" that is increasingly reconstituted in scientific terms that are themselves the mix of multiple disciplinary and moralizing perspectives.[33] It is an "explicitly hybrid project" that is the triumph of medicalization along with psychology, social work, public health, and criminology.[34] The people who are called on to respond to addiction, not as a single entity but rather in its myriad, and often-conflicting manifestations, reinforce this hybridity.

While habitual substance use is widely considered the disease of addiction, the limits to this construction are most apparent when the focus shifts to the *treatment* of this disease. As the sociologist Carl May explains, medical constructions engage moral questions precisely because addiction can be known only through its symptoms—behaviors considered abnormal—rather than any specific clinical sign that exists independent of this behavior. While clinical theories that rely on the "neuroscience" of addiction are beginning to dominate how we understand habitual substance use, addiction is apparent only through the behavior of the individual and, importantly, through the individual's description of what they are experiencing. This has resulted in a "quasi-disease model of addiction," where the emphasis is on behavior as a sign of the disease.[35] This behavioral focus affects what it means to treat the disease that can only be known through these behaviors. The disease model, then, is what Carl May calls a "discursive device," which explains loss of control in the face of no scientific evidence to measure this phenomenon. Physicians, when confronted with an addict, are dependent on the symptoms of addiction, as expressed by the addict, and are required, through a conflation, to turn these symptoms into clinical signs of a disease. In the absence of clinical signs, the addict's feelings about her or his substance use become the evidence that is used to create the diagnosis.

The difficulty, then, is twofold for the physician. First, the physician must rely on the patient to express symptoms of a disease that has no clinical indicators beyond those symptoms. Second, the physician is required to treat a condition whose cure—abstinence—requires, again, the patient's willpower to effect recovery because the physician has little to offer in the way of treatment. While there has been a trend toward identifying addiction as a social problem of medicine, the medical field finds addiction difficult to understand and especially difficult to treat. As May concludes, addiction, then, becomes a problem *of* medicine—it is a disease created by physicians—and *for* medicine—doctors can't cure the disease their field has helped create.

Combined, the historical and contemporary work on the medicalization of addiction correctly emphasizes the trend toward understanding habitual substance use as a disease amenable to some sort of treatment, regardless of whether medical professionals are directly involved in that treatment. However, by emphasizing the predominance of the disease model of addiction, scholars interested in this approach tend to de-emphasize, or ignore, the limits to the medical model of addiction. These limits are twofold: first, by focusing on medical conceptions of how one becomes an addict, these scholars ignore the extent to which, at the level of treatment, the medicalization of addiction is, at best, incomplete. Second, these scholars, by seeking evidence for the medicalization of addiction, tend to downplay the second predominant way drugs and drug use have been conceptualized over the twentieth and twenty-first centuries in the United States, namely, through their criminalization.

The specific modalities offered in the drug treatment system are not properly medicalized from the institutional or interactional perspective. Addiction treatment in the United States is still dominated by the approach established by Alcoholics Anonymous, which posits addiction as a disease but explicitly eschews the role of medical professionals in treatment, preferring to use the broad label "self-help" as the approach best suited to achieving abstinence from drugs. It is a model that relies, ironically, on discourses of freedom to explain compulsive relationships to alcohol: addicts liberate themselves and become free from compulsion by exerting their willpower over their destructive impulses. In this model, addiction is a disease of the will more so than one of the brain or of behavior; it is cured through willpower rather than medicine or therapy.[36]

The one arena in which medicalized interventions dominate drug treatment is with "replacement therapies" that mimic, either fully or partially, the effect of the "unacceptable" (and usually illegal) drug to which one is addicted. Methadone, introduced as a treatment for opiate addiction, is perhaps the most prominent example of this type of treatment. It is also subject to considerable controversy, with opponents, many from competing abstinence-based treatment programs, arguing that it replaces one addiction with another. Describing methadone in 1973, the sociologist Dorothy Elkin wrote that "the controversy over methadone maintenance reflects the tangle of often irreconcilable legal, moral, political, and medical attitudes toward addiction and its treatment"—an observation that remains salient today.[37] These contradictory views were brought to bear on methadone's system of distribution in significant ways. Initially intended as a maintenance drug to be distributed by physicians, potentially for the duration of the addict's life, federal guidelines developed by the Food and Drug Administration and state regulations—influenced heavily by methadone opponents—severely restricted its distribution.[38] Methadone clinics, operating in a "bureaucratic jungle" of federal and state guidelines, are subject to considerable oversight from regulatory agencies, which has greatly affected the nature of the setting in which methadone is distributed. Methadone patients must adhere to strict rules for obtaining the drug, which some have argued are more punitive than therapeutic in nature.[39] For example, people seeking methadone must go to the clinic daily (or several times a week), take the drug while being observed by clinic staff, provide urine for random drug screenings, and meet with clinic counselors. There can be high levels of distrust between patients and the staff, responsible for both maintaining strict rules and providing "therapy" to clients who have little say over their course of treatment. The result is a setting where punitive and medical perspectives come together in an "unhappy compromise" for people receiving methadone.[40] As one drug policy reformer and former methadone user I spoke with explained, "Methadone turns us into desexualized fucking children." Another has referred to methadone as "liquid handcuffs," providing some relief from heroin dependence at the cost of much social control.

Others have argued for a more complicated view of methadone's function in drug users' lives. Drawing on the philosopher Jacques Derrida's notion of the pharmakon—drug as both antidote and poison, existing within regimes of prohibition and liberalization[41]—the sociologists Suzanne Fraser and kylie valentine view methadone as a complicated phenomenon, rather than a substance, that through its discourses and practices allows some addicts the freedom to feel normal even while placing them in a "uniquely marginal social location."[42] They are marginal because they are no longer the fantasy outlaw heroin user but neither are they its counterpart, the sober addict. Depictions of the compliant methadone user, disciplined through this highly regulated management of his or her heroin addiction, fail to account for how some methadone users engaged with this treatment in ways that resist the binary of oppositional heroin addict versus docile methadone user. This complicated view of methadone is justified because of its fraught social, legal, cultural, and political significance. Methadone and other replacement therapies are never just drugs or medicine: they are continually recast in the normative and prescriptive (rather than medical) frameworks that constitute our theories of addiction.

Because addiction and its treatment are social, legal, moral, normative, and prescriptive categories whose meanings are unstable, they are often subject to contradictory regimes of oversight that reflect their unstable definitions. Conrad and Schneider argue that because of the large governmental involvement in methadone and its system of distribution, methadone treatment was never justified on a theoretical level by a well-developed disease model and was complicated by these competing legal and regulatory discourses.[43] To date, methadone remains extremely controversial and underused in comparison with other treatment modalities. According to data collected about admissions to publicly funded drug treatment programs, the majority of people who enroll in drug treatment for primary opiate addiction do not receive replacement therapies as a part of their treatment plan.[44] With programs such as drug courts, the vast majority of treatment programs utilized are behaviorally focused and abstinence-based, and in most drug courts defendants on replacement therapies cannot enroll in court-supervised treatment until they are "drug-free."[45] One of my interviewees explained judicial resistance to methadone this way: "Who wants someone drooling in the courtroom and nodding off when everyone else has to be clean?"

While addiction is referred to as a "disease," the institutional context for its treatment is a reminder of the limits of the medical model. These limits are evident even within the institutions most concerned with advancing the disease model of compulsive substance. While the National Institute on Drug Abuse argues that addiction is a neurobiological disorder, they also are not averse to coercion. In their document titled "Thirteen Principles of Effective Drug Addiction Treatment," principle 10 explains that "treatment does not need to be voluntary to be effective," and that "sanctions or enticements . . . in the criminal justice system can significantly increase treatment entry, retention and success."[46]

The cycles of conscience and convenience that motivate punishment reformers are directly influenced by the prevailing theories about behavior that come from outside the realm of punishment generally, and the criminal justice system more specifically. While religious concerns motivated colonial era efforts to contain deviance, and social work and sociological theories predominated during Progressive Era criminal justice reforms, today's problem-solving courts draw largely on medical and behavioral theories of deviance. These theories emphasize the individual as the source of deviance and advocate interventions, often coerced, that attempt to fix the sick individual. These quasi-medical theories give drug courts their particular, and unique, logic. However, drug courts are part of a longer historical efforts to ascribe a type of determinism to deviance, and to use prevailing theories to cure this deviance, in an attempt to counter arguments that crime stems from an individual's free will.

That drug courts draw on medicalized theories of addiction makes sense given the dominance of the disease discourse in conceptualizations of habitual substance use. Yet, by drawing on these medicalized interpretations to advocate for enhanced criminal justice, rather than medical, oversight of drug users, drug courts are directly contributing to the medicalization of addiction in a key way. The alternative to medicalization is often presented as "demedicalization," where the emphasis on illness and the doctor's role in curing this illness is replaced by alternative understandings of deviance that de-emphasize the medical model's hold in explaining the phenomena in question.[47] Drug courts, and coerced therapeutic sanctions generally, represent a third approach, which constitutes the *appropriation* of medicalization that simultaneously emphasizes the veracity of the disease model while de-emphasizing the hold the medical system should have on curing the problem.

This appropriation is accomplished through the adoption of behavioral theories of recovery that eschew medicalized perspectives at the level of treatment, and allow for myriad other approaches, broadly characterized as punitive and rehabilitative. In the next chapter, I show how drug court advocates move from this emphasis on addiction as a "genuine neurobiological disease of the brain," to the conclusion that "force is the best medicine" when arguing for the important role that coercion can, and should, play in curing addiction. By focusing on the behavioral manifestation of the disease of addiction, and crafting an intervention meant to alter the disease's outward form, drug courts fit within the progression of punitive interventions that aim to cure deviance and promote conformity.

5

"Force Is the Best Medicine"

Addiction, Recovery, and Coercion

The rising toll of substance abuse and addiction is undeniable and poses the greatest threat to our domestic welfare.
—C. West Huddleston, NADCP Director

Introduction

Drug court advocates attempt to reframe the focus of the court toward the healing function they so clearly believe is in the court's power to achieve by drawing on theories outside the criminal justice system about the nature of addiction and its effective treatment. They use these theories to argue for the benefits of coerced treatment over imprisonment of drug users and voluntary treatment. In doing so, they make their case that the courts are the ideal site within which to enact the change necessary to transform addicts' lives.

Drug court advocates conceive of addiction in both medical and moral terms. The moral terms are most apparent when they describe the qualities of the addict, constructed as faults, and how to best change these qualities. Their constructions of what addicts are like and how they can be transformed lend themselves directly to particular types of intervention centered on force and coercion. Force becomes a defining feature of interventions designed to instill "consequential thinking" in people so "dope sick" that they are unable to plan for the future.

By constructing addicts as requiring force, drug court advocates focus on sanctions, their particular brand of force that has become the hallmark of the drug court practice. Advocates' strong endorsement of sanctions—"where the rubber hits the road"—is tied directly to their theories of recovery from addiction. Sanctions provide the link between recovery and punishment that allows advocates to speak of punishment's healing, rather than merely vindictive, function. By emphasizing addicts' need for understanding the consequences of addiction, "accountability" becomes a central feature of drug court advocates' notions of what exactly the court is instilling in drug court defendants. Drug court advocates use several terms to describe people going through drug courts, including defendant, participant, and client. This differential labeling speaks to the seemingly contradictory approach at the heart of sanctions, especially ones that lead to jail or prison. To view a person as simultaneously a defendant and a client masks the fact that they are, for legal purposes, the former.

By focusing on the need for accountability and "swift and certain responses to noncompliance," drug court advocates make their case not only for coerced treatment, which has been in existence for several decades in the United States, but specifically for the role of the judge as the person best equipped to act quickly and meaningfully to address drug court participants' transgressions. As a "moral authority" the judge is framed as the person best equipped to oversee treatment, both because of the power vested in him or her through the social position accorded this profession, and because of the emotional and potentially therapeutic power vested in the judge via his or her interaction with the defendant.

The goals of drug courts link directly to drug court advocates' theories of addiction and recovery, and to their broader goals for institutional transformation within the criminal justice system. The extremely broad criteria used by some drug courts to determine a defendant's readiness to "graduate" reflect both encompassing theories of addiction recovery and greatly enhanced goals for the court. These theories and goals reflect moral considerations that extend far beyond the clinical "facts" of addiction or the legal "facts" of the case that brought the defendant under the criminal justice system's jurisdiction in the first place.

Drug court advocates construct theories of addiction and its treatment that give the courts a preferred role in curing addiction. They are interested in retaining the criminal justice system's hold on an illness whose primary manifestation is in behaviors deemed relevant to the courts, and whose cure is recognized, again, through behavioral markers that are of direct relevance to an expanding criminal justice system.

Theories of Addiction and Recovery

Drug court advocates call their work "enlightened coercion," enlightened because they're drawing on what proponents call the "psychopharmacological science" or, alternatively, the "neuroscience of addiction."[1] As one advocate explained:

> Neuroscience has come so far in the last ten years that unless you're a Neanderthal you'll understand what the science tells you about the hijacked brain, which is a term out of NIDA and the effects that drugs have . . . the effects that [these] drugs have on the pleasure centers of the brain and one's inability to ultimately get off of those drugs without long-term assistance and intensive assistance and treatment. The point is that the neuroscience is just such strong evidence that there is a biological impact and that treatment is necessary to get this individual's neurochemistry restored. And that it takes a great deal of time.

As another advocate explained when I asked him to describe addiction, "It's a brain disease. End of story." Most advocates I spoke with referred, broadly, to the "disease model of addiction" as being central to the formation of drug courts, yet few could describe addiction's disease-like qualities in much detail. They seemed less interested in defining addiction as a disease than in pointing out that it is because of societal acceptance of the disease model that the public has supported drug courts and other rehabilitative sanctions.[2] As one interviewee explained:

> Drug courts are unimaginable without this growing assumption that . . . addiction is a disease that can be treated. Right? So there's two assumptions there. That it's a disease and that it can be treated. And that's a growing assumption; those assumptions are not just operating within the criminal justice system. Those are social assumptions that are larger than the criminal justice system, or larger than the judiciary. . . . I think it's a generally held assumption.

As an article introducing drug courts explains:

> A necessary feature of drug treatment courts is the definition of drug use as a disease rather than a criminal offense, a departure from the justice

system's past stance. This results, in part, from a therapeutic culture that interprets many forms of deviance as treatable sickness. Within this cultural context and faced with a legal system that has not worked to control drug use, it is understandable that judges have embraced a treatment approach.[3]

Again, without describing what exactly the disease model is, another advocate explained that "there's a general knowledge that you gather living your life. . . . You read articles, I mean it's not just the criminal justice system that has adopted the disease model. I think society has come a long way." Overall, drug courts are possible because of a widespread "recognition that the system had absolutely failed . . . coupled with a growing, certainly not universal, but growing acceptance of the disease model." As someone else pointed out, "It used to be we locked people up for being alcoholics . . . and, finally, we said, alcoholism is a disease. . . . And I think the culture has changed . . . and I'm seeing it with drug addiction. I'm seeing more of . . . the medical model."

Despite using disease language to describe addiction, calling it an illness, and saying drug court defendants are sick, for the most part drug court proponents have little to say about the nature of the disease. One of the only physicians involved with drug courts nationally attributes the strength of drug courts to the fact that drug courts "don't let people hide behind their disease," explaining further:

[Drug courts] basically recognize that addiction is not a disease and it's not one to be approached in a purely medical way. What I mean by that is with a passive patient . . . it's in your brain because of course you use a drug and it's going to affect your serotonin and dopamine system, OK, but now what? It's primarily a social problem, it's people who don't know how to negotiate the stresses of everyday life. . . . I suppose that it straddles psychology and social problems, but I consider it more of a social problem.

While this particular advocate presented a view of addiction that was unlike the way other advocates talked about addiction, this perspective actually corresponds to the way drug court advocates presented the advantages of drug courts over traditional case processing and over voluntary drug treatment. Overall, drug court advocates are less concerned that people are sick and far more concerned with how their sickness manifests itself, namely, in "antisocial," not necessarily just criminal, behavior.

It is at the level of treatment that drug courts actually make their intervention, and they make judicially enforced coercion the key feature of that intervention. One of the ways they make this case for coercion is by focusing less on the etiology of the disease of addiction and far more on what this disease does to the "character" of the person afflicted by it. An important way that addiction is known, paradoxically, is through the denial of its presence by the addicted person. This is because, according to most of the people I spoke with, addicts derive too much pleasure from their addiction, refuse to admit they are addicted, and will stop using drugs only if they are forced to. And when addicts say they want to be cured, they can't necessarily be trusted, because they will "lie like crazy" to keep using illegal substances. As one interviewee explained:

> We always say to [addicts] "I don't believe a thing you say." . . . [Addicts] lie so convincingly . . . they're just good at it. The question is, are they lying because they're addicts or were they always liars? And, I think in a lot of cases, look, this is them. This is their character and that's what you want to help change because even if they don't use drugs anymore, if they lie on the job about various things or they're dishonest in relationships, they're not going to be happy, so it's an across the board quality to work on.

This advocate expressed an important point—the goal of drug courts, in part, is to help people be "happy," with sobriety as a step toward this happiness. Because addicts lie to keep using drugs, they require heavy monitoring, because you can't "leave it in the person's lap to convince you that they're motivated, that they're doing what they say they're going to do. . . . I mean, they're just good at [lying]." One of the reasons addicts lie is because they're "driven by their addictions," but their addiction renders them "so drug stupid that they make easy arrests or become easy arrests." Arrest, then, becomes an "opportunity" for people who are "broken by addiction" and who have a strong "thirst for sobriety" but little motivation to enter or complete treatment. Arrest "allows the criminal justice system to become the therapeutic change agent by pushing the offender into treatment rather than jail."[4] Drug courts offer "the coercive power to get people into treatment who don't want it. And to keep people there who don't want to stay there." Importantly, drug courts "teach people to learn to manage their ambivalence toward recovery." Drug courts, then, rely on the criminalization of drugs, of which policing is a crucial part. While their motivation for starting drug courts, as detailed in chapter 3, was to change the way "business is done" with drug users, they rely on that business, the criminalization of drug use and heavy policing of drug users, for their intervention.

One of the reasons that addicts make such easy arrests, according to this logic, is that their addiction renders them unable to think beyond their immediate need to use drugs. Several advocates I interviewed talked about drug users as if they were children who needed to be taught to think like adults. As one person explained, echoing a prevailing sentiment:

Well, it's like kids. . . . Addicts go through their addicted lives thinking their drug use will have no consequences. They can continue to use drugs and they won't lose their health, they won't lose their partner, they won't lose their children, they won't lose their job, they won't lose their home. And they really believe this, notwithstanding all evidence to the contrary. Because they don't think consequentially.

An article on drug courts explains that addicts have "profound problems of self-governance" that require "limit-setting, consistency and firmness."[5] Its author goes on to explain:

Some psychological traits are fairly typical of addicts; among them (1) low tolerance for stress and emotional turmoil, and (2) poor behavioral control. . . . Such traits and associated features are likely manifested as poor impulse control, inability to delay gratification, action-oriented (rather than reflection), poor ability to plan and anticipate consequences of actions, misreading of interpersonal situations and damaged capacity to trust.[6]

The job of the court is to teach addicts to think consequentially, and the way the court does this is by attempting to foster a sense of "accountability . . . to the court system but ultimately accountability to themselves and their families." This idea of accountability and taking responsibility for one's actions is an important part of drug courts and at the heart of how drug court advocates explain the purpose of this coercive practice. A primer on problem-solving courts explains that they start with "the premise that people should be held accountable for their harmful behavior."[7] Addicts, according to an interviewee, "need accountability . . . not to play games. To have someone say, 'you want to do this, you've got a problem.'" Drug court, explained another interviewee, "combines accountability with treatment. And without that, well, treatment is better than something but not much." In other words, treatment will work only if addicts are coerced.

To foster accountability, addicts need to see, to be shown, that repeated drug use has consequences. These consequences come in the form of "personally meaningful" sanctions and incentives imposed by a judge vested with the "moral authority" and legal backing to carry them out. Drug court advocates actively construct a solution to the problem of addiction, with coercion as the centerpiece and an expanded role for courts, and judges specifically, in the recovery process.

Sanctions and Incentives

Sanctions and incentives are central to drug court practice. As one advocate explained, "There's probably no more important subject. . . . How do you respond to good behavior and bad?" A prominent drug court researcher explains, "There's no room for debate: the application of swift, certain and appropriately modulated sanctions and rewards improves behavior over time."[8] There is no room to debate because sanctions and incentives are the heart of the drug court model—to argue against them would be to argue with the fundamental ideology of coerced treatment. Everyone I interviewed extolled the virtue of sanctions and incentives, basing it largely on their uniformly held view that addicts will not stop using drugs unless compelled to with rewards and punishment. As one person explained, "Addicts need carrots, they need sticks, in order to stay about new behaviors [sic]." They need "swift and certain consequences" to their misbehavior. "You don't punish a child for something they did six months ago because it will have absolutely no impact on their behavior. You have a dirty urine, you will have a sanction today . . . the immediacy of the response. . . . So, your bad behavior will have consequences." The immediacy is important because "just the threat of some long-term bad thing happening to them" will not serve as enough of a deterrent to drug use; rather, "the immediacy of sanctions . . . is a great behavior changer."

The "formalized system of sanctions and rewards" is considered essential to effective drug court practice.[9] It is justified by reference to "behavioral research" and "science" as to what motivates people to change. As one article on drug courts explains:

> Every dirty urine drug screen or missed appointment is met with a sanction, with the severity of these sanctions escalating if infractions recur. This conforms to what behaviorists have long appreciated, that behavior is shaped most effectively when punishment are swift and sure.... The strategy demonstrates to the participant that his actions are taken seriously and that he predictably controls his fate.[10]

While drug court defendants are heavily monitored by the courts and treatment providers, they are also reminded that they "control their fate" through their decisions about their drug use. Despite this freedom, they cannot chose to use drugs without sometimes-severe consequences. Jail, the ultimate symbol of a punitive sanction and one that many advocates spoke against as a blanket approach to drug users, becomes a "treatment tool" when meted out as a sanction by drug courts. One advocate referred to it as "motivational jail" because it is meant to encourage the defendant to strive for sobriety. Short jail sentences, or "flash incarceration," for treatment failures serve to remind the defendant that the "court means business." A drug court practitioner fact sheet titled "The Critical Need for Jail as a Sanction in the Drug Court Model" explains that jail sentences can be "instrumental in the change in behavior among drug court participants."[11]

To become enlightened about behavior change, drug court advocates draw on psychological and behavioral studies, some conducted on nonhuman animals, to develop a complex system of sanctions and rewards that is systematic yet personalized.[12] The personalized system is key, according to advocates, "if you're going to truly reward them and if you're going to truly punish them, know them, and do things that are meaningful and impactful to them."

Drug court judges and staff learn about what is important to individual defendants and use this personal knowledge to devise punishments and rewards that will help them become "sober and law-abiding." Drug courts, then, ask defendants to trust them by giving personal information that then can be used to help punish them for infractions and reward them for accomplishments. As one advocate explained, "Responses are in the eye of the behaver [sic]. Giving me Yankees tickets as a reward is not a reward to me. I'm not a Yankees fan. It's a punishment. So know your clients." Another person I interviewed, who has conducted several studies on drug court effectiveness, explained that "graduated sanctions and rewards that motivate behavior . . . tangible rewards and punishments" are high on the list of what ensures drug court success. According to another advocate, considerations such as "Am I going to jail or not? Am I going to be able to see my kids? Am I going to have my child support payments reduced so that I can earn enough money to live? Am I going to find a place to live and is somebody going to help me with my health problem? Is somebody going to help me with my psychological problem?" all figure into transforming the addict's behavior.

The strength of drug court comes, in part, from enacting personalized sanctions and incentives in a "swift and coordinated way." Drug court success stems from:

> the very, very strict fact that people . . . know what's expected of them and what's going to happen if they don't do it. So whatever it is that could be a consequence of not following through is likely going to happen. This is just the first order of business. It's the consequences and all this other stuff is window dressing and it makes them feel good, they're being therapeutic.

The punishment for failing to comply must be one that sufficiently motivates the drug court defendant to adhere to the prescribed treatment plan.

While sanctions and rewards are essential to drug court practice, advocates stress the need for a graduated system. This comes back to the nature of addiction and the widespread understanding of it as a "chronic, relapsing condition." An article on drug courts explains:

> A fundamental underpinning of drug treatment courts is that "drug abuse" is a chronic, relapsing condition and that an offender may "slip" up or relapse several times during treatment. Efforts are made to keep noncompliant offenders in the program, using rewards such as encouragement from the judge, or small tokens, and sanctions such as community service or a weekend in jail. A wider range of rewards and sanctions are therefore available in drug treatment court.[13]

In a document published by the National Drug Court Association ti-tled "Defining Drug Court: The Key Components," component 6 (of 10) explains that "an established principle of AOD [alcohol and other drug] treatment is that addiction is a chronic, relapsing condition. . . . Becoming sober or drug free is a learning experience and each relapse to AOD use may teach something about the recovery process."[14] For this reason, courts must be prepared with a "coordinated strategy that governs drug courts' response to participants' compliance."

According to advocates, it is this understanding of the "inevitability" or the "great likelihood of relapse" that has been an important part of the shift in understanding of the courts, and judges specifically. Prior to drug courts, as one advocate explained, "the courts didn't understand that re-lapse is part of the deal." Because drug court advocates and practitioners view relapse as an inevitable and integral part of addiction, frequent moni-toring by the drug court staff is considered essential. Without this moni-toring, a defendant's relapse cannot be identified and the "swift and cer-tain" consequences for repeated drug use cannot be implemented in the graduated way that advocates uniformly believe compels motivated defen-dants to stop using drugs.

Highly personalized information is collected about the defendants to ensure that they are at least striving to remain drug-free. Urine screening forms a central part of drug court practice and serves as one important way that compliance with treatment is monitored. But urine screening is just one part of the process where detailed information about the defen-dant can be reviewed by all drug court staff. As an article comparing the implementation of drug court practice with traditional case processing explains:

> Drug treatment courts . . . emphasize a detailed and more interpretive review of criminal histories, numerous screening for case eligibility, and formal substance abuse assessment which typically include information regarding the extent and nature of drug use, employment history, educa-tional achievement, living arrangements and family history.[15]

As drug court defendants are supervised:

> their progress in treatment is reviewed by numerous persons on the drug court team. All drug court team members have the opportunity to review

and interpret information on participants' backgrounds and progress. On multiple occasions . . . we observed prosecutors, defense attorneys, and judges analyzing treatment progress reports, urinalysis results, and risk factors that were traditionally beyond the purview of the case supervision decisions.[16]

Additional information collected included "details of the offenders' lives—their childhood traumas, parents' drug use, educational experiences and histories and patterns of drug use."[17] Drug court defendants' lives are examined with far greater scrutiny than traditional processing would entail, all in the name of facilitating their recovery.

Because of the nature of both addiction, with the inevitability of relapse, and addicts, who are liars and reluctant to stop using drugs, this personal information is considered necessary for the drug court to effectively do its job. Drug courts are attempting to undo the backlash against the misuse of discretion by arguing for its necessity in curing addiction and stopping drug-related crime. But drug court advocates are not just arguing for the increased use of mandated treatment in general. They craft a specific argument that places the judge at the head of a team that is, in the end, only as effective as its leader. Here we get to the heart of the drug court model. Drug courts use theories of addiction, such as the inevitability of relapse, and behavioral theories about the importance of sanctions and rewards, to craft a system where the judge is the crucial figure. Because of the authority bestowed on judges, they are the only people who can enact coerced drug treatment in a way that has any chance of being truly effective.

"The Power of the Robe"

The judge is considered the "symbolic and functional centerpiece of the drug court program."[18] As one advocate explained, "The judge is able to keep people engaged in the therapeutic process better than anyone else. . . . The judge, when enlightened and when trained, is unstoppable." The judge, then, is more effective than a therapist or doctor at curing addiction. The judge represents a "moral authority. . . . The expression of the participant's psychological conflicts and needs naturally find outlet in a setting where a potent figure actively probes for personal details and takes visible interest in their lives."[19] The personalized nature of the interaction between the judge and the defendant is uniformly extolled by drug courts advocates as the key to these courts' success.

Tying into the idea that addicts are like children, the judge assumes a parental role in the defendant's life. As one advocate explained:

> The key piece of the drug court is the regular and frequent interaction between the court and the participant. And what happens, every focus group that's been done with participants, if you ask them what mattered most in their succeeding, they'll say the judge. And they become vested in the judge's approval, in an authority figure caring about them. They love their judges, it doesn't matter if they're men, women, young, old, dynamic, sleepers. It just doesn't matter. They all cite the judge as important.

Another advocate elaborated on this dynamic:

> There's a parental relationship or dynamic that appears to occur with some defendants in court. Where a defendant or participant in drug court really doesn't want to let that judge down. There's something parental that goes on. And there's some kind of transference that goes on there, where somebody truly an authority and truly respected in the community is rooting for the participant. And we've interviewed hundreds of graduates and just anecdotally . . . they'll say that the judge believed in me, they saw something positive in me that I didn't see in myself for a period of time.

In the drug court, the judge plays an authoritative role, but he or she is also supposed to tap into the therapeutic potential of this authority. As one advocate explained it, "The judge is really crucial because it's a different type of judging. . . . Maybe someday it will be traditional, but it's a nontraditional role. . . . It's a lot of social work, a lot of cheerleader, coach, mentor. . . . It takes a different type of person. The judge has to have a different role." Further:

> When you're in front of the judge, it's a privilege. . . . And you have to perform. There's a bonding process. . . . The men and women that are judges, whether they're appointed or elected, are revered in our society. They're the ones who . . . well, we know it's not true, they don't all have special knowledge, and they're not all pristine and pure, but they are in our

minds. Our society looks to judges [as] one of the few vestiges of public service that we still continually respect. . . . Overall, the general public has an acceptance that they will hear things, that they will work harder, try to please more a man or woman wearing a black robe.

As one judge explained:

> I think the personal involvement of the judge is the cornerstone of the drug court. Without it, I don't think that our mission can be accomplished. . . . I think it is important for offenders to have a relationship with the judge and to know that if they aren't compliant the judge will be angry. If something has gone on in their lives that created pain, the judge will be sad. If they are successful, the judge will respond to that positively. I do think the personal involvement is critical to the participant's success.[20]

As another person has explained, of the personalized approach of drug courts:

> For example, a standard question we ask of addicts in our program is: "Who in your life can help you?" That becomes a trigger to say, "Do you think the next time you come before me, your girlfriend can come with you?" When that girlfriend comes, we say, "Wow, this must be difficult for you. What are some of the things you'd like to see happen?" You literally turn that girlfriend into your ally and into a long-term source of support for the offender, by engaging her in the intervention.[21]

Part of the dominant view of addiction is that it affects all facets of one's life, including relationships with family, friends, and peers. For this reason, while adult drug courts are punishing the criminal act of one individual, they view the individual's social relationships as implicitly part of their punishment/treatment. The courts enlist family members, friends, and others in this therapeutic project; the courts' jurisdiction expands in the name of helping people. Because it's done for the defendant's own good, this expanding surveillance receives no scrutiny by advocates, and instead is lauded as the right way to deal with offenders and a sign of the courts' concern.

While some advocates talked about the emotional response the judge evokes in the defendant, others pointed to the power the judge has, institutionally, as the reason drug courts can succeed. As one person explained, "Who is more powerful in the criminal justice system than the judge?" Other forms of coerced treatment are ineffective because "they just didn't have the juice behind them like a drug court judge does." It's the "power of the robe" that drug court advocates identify as a key attribute of drug court success. As one advocate explained, "Judges, rightly or wrongly, hold a very special place. Courts hold a very special place in American society. And I think you can use the clout or the leverage of the court to do immense good." The impetus for judges to get involved in drug courts, according to one person I interviewed:

> was the desire to tilt the scales back to judicial discretion and judicial authority and away from prosecutorial authority. There's plenty of diversion programs that prosecutors control both the purse strings and the hammer. I think there was a desire of judges to get in on the action and see if they could achieve better results.

Judges achieve these "better results" because they have the power to enact sanctions swiftly and with consequences. Departing from the general enthusiasm conveyed by most advocates I spoke with about the "transference" or personalized relationship between the judge and the defendant, one interviewee brought the judge's effectiveness back to his or her power to enact graduated sanctions, the "tangible rewards and punishments." This interviewee attributed the success of drug courts to the judge's authority, backed by the threat of jail, rather than "this relationship which is, for most people, three minutes maybe every third week." Force, according to this perspective, is the most important part of drug courts. The threat of jail, then, becomes the key factor in recovery.

Curing an Incurable Disease

The judge is at the head of the team that uses carrots and sticks, and perhaps parental role-playing, to cure the addicts/defendants/participants who come before the court. The challenge for drug courts, then, becomes determining what it means for addicts to be cured. This is especially difficult in light of theories about addiction that have relapse as a key feature of the disease the court is trying to cure. In addition, by having to cure addiction, courts are reorienting themselves toward the future action of defendants rather than solely punishing a past act. As one advocate explained:

> The court in a drug court model uses its coercive power to try to support and move participants successfully through their recovery. And that's clearly not a traditional role for the courts. Courts traditionally are focused on process. They explicitly have no interest and in fact think it unethical to have any interest in the outcome of the case. They are there to adjudicate past facts by and large, past actions, and have no interest in guilt, innocence, what a jury finds, what the outcome is. Their job is to . . . adjudicate past facts, fashion appropriate punishment where appropriate, and be sure that the process occurs in a way that is legally and constitutionally mandated. So traditional courts are about process. Problem-solving courts are about the exact opposite, in a sense. Their ultimate goal is to change the future behavior of the litigants, and in drug courts that is certainly true, and to preserve public safety and community safety and so forth. But they are very focused on changing the litigant's behavior.

One way they justify this expansion is through references to the health of not just individuals but communities. An introductory reader on problem-solving courts explains that they "extend the role of the legal system beyond fact-finding and the imposition of sanctions. They use the authority of the court to maintain the social health of the community."[22] Further, "Problem-solving courts are moving the legal system away from the bureaucratic, state-centered perspective and toward a framework that sees each court embedded in the community from which it draws its clientele."[23] Because of this focus on the community, "problem-solving courts tend not to confine their reformist energies to the four walls of the courthouse . . . [but] also seek to achieve broader goals in the community at large, using their prestige to affect [sic] change outside the court-room without comprising [sic] the integrity of the judicial process within the courtroom."[24] Marilyn Roberts, a staff member for the U.S. Department of Justice office that oversees drug courts, explained their role this way:

> Another issue is the question of where treatment begins and ends. Drug courts have expanded the concept of treatment beyond its traditional definition. With drug courts the goal is not simply to get participants sober,

as it might be in a straight-up treatment program, because then you just end up with a sober criminal. The idea is to work on the behavior that is problematic to the community. So for drug courts the goal is not just sobriety but also law-abiding behavior.[25]

Addiction, from the drug court perspective, is a disease that is rooted in the individual but whose symptoms affect the community. These symptoms—namely, criminal behavior—can occur even when the disease is in remission; so the questions becomes, what exactly would mean success for a drug court?

What Is the Cure?

Drug courts are concerned, principally, with "abstinence from drugs," but their challenge is how to foster this abstinence and its long-term maintenance.[26] Although one advocate said there is "one mission, to get this person clean and sober," other advocates disagreed. As another advocate explained, "It's not good to just to get somebody clean and sober. We might as well have done nothing if that's all we've done." Drug courts are interested in affecting a constellation of behaviors believed to contribute to drug use and its outgrowth, criminal activity. They become, as one advocate called them, "a resocialization process." These courts are in the business of "personality changing." They are focused on transforming the defendant's "character" because, as one advocate explained, drug treatment is not so much about rehabilitation as *habilitation*; the goals is to instill in addicts values they may have never encountered before. The same community they're a menace to is also, ironically, the one that never taught them the right values. Drug courts "fix folks" by habilitating them to the values of drug court proponents.

It is at the level of the goals of drug courts, what it means to actually "fix" someone, that moral and medical considerations merge quite clearly. It is also at this level that we see a large amount of discretion on the part of the drug court judge and staff emerge. As an advocate explained, "For an addict, we're asking them to change everything—their friendships, how they see themselves in the world, their family dynamic, their hangouts, down to the music they listen to and how they dress." Another proponent explained:

> We've got to make sure they can work, that they're educated, that they can get a job, that they can keep a job, that they have skills, that they . . . learn how to get up in the morning and go to work. That they learn that when their boss pisses them off they don't slug them. That they learn behavior they've never learned before. How do you get a house, how do you raise your kids? . . . If you don't have a kind of holistic view of this person's recovery, you're setting these people up for failure.

Advocates' theories of what it takes to facilitate recovery—what aspects of the defendant's/client's/participant's lives need to be in place for recovery to take hold—are quite broad. The court, then, becomes concerned with behaviors that aren't necessarily illegal but over which courts stake their claim in the name of recovery. The courts do this because these behaviors are considered to be both affected *by* addiction and ones that behavioral theories claim are necessary for recovery *from* addiction.

Ironically, despite drug court being an explicitly coercive model, some people justify the court's expanded jurisdiction by the fact that participants choose to enter court-mandated treatment. As John Schwartz, the chief judge of Rochester City Court, where defendants are required to get a GED and have a job before they graduate, explained in a roundtable on the role of drug courts in reintegration:

> I see less of a need to establish limits on the court's authority when participation is voluntary. In our court, defendants have a choice: you can go into the regular court system and be prosecuted, or you can go into drug court. Having signed a contract for the drug court, you have sold your soul to me for the natural jurisdiction of our court—five years for a felony, three for a misdemeanor. You have to comply with the program or I'll impose sanctions, including jail.[27]

The National Association of Drug Court Professionals, in a document outlining the key components of drug courts, argues that a drug court program's effectiveness should be measured according to the following outcomes: reduced recidivism rates, abstinence from drugs and alcohol, changes in jobs skills and employment, changes in literacy and educational attainment, changes in physical and mental health, changes in the status of family relationships, increased use of health care and other social services, and increased economic productivity. It is these factors that determine whether a particular court has been effective and against which drug court performance should be measured.[28]

Karen Freeman-Wilson, a retired drug court judge and former CEO of the National Association of Drug Court Professionals, has argued before the U.S. Congress that traditional measures of court success such as recidivism rates are insufficient to measure the transformations drug courts are seeking.[29] Rather, Judge Freeman-Wilson argued, drug court participants, in order to be considered successful, should be "required to engage in community service, actively search for a job, comply with ancillary services they may have been sent to and tak[e] prescribed medication for co-occurring disorders." Further, she explained, the courts should examine the drug court defendant's relationship with family members and ask, "Is this person developing new, healthy relationships?" And follow-up measures of success should examine the participant's "pro-social participation in the community. How do they give back?"

The Center for Court Innovation—an organization based in New York City that has funded and evaluated drug courts in New York State and has made substantial contributions to the national discussion about problem-solving courts generally[30]—argues for the importance of "extending the judge's authority," writing that "perhaps some of the basic elements of aftercare—looking for a job, getting an education, coming up with a plan for housing, family reunification" should be part of the last phase of court supervision. If this were the case, they argue, "judges could then bring the coercive power of the court to this aspect of recovery, pushing clients towards a firm hold on a stable life and withholding graduation until at least some basics are in place."[31]

Drug courts broaden the scope of activities the court monitors, in the name of helping people, and draw on prevailing theories of addiction and recovery to justify their expanded jurisdiction. As one advocate explained, "Drug courts become very personal. Drug court judges become very involved with these people. The clinical people do. The defense does. The prosecutors do. They *care* about these people. And when you care about people, you want to do more and more and more for them."

In my interviews, I asked about the potential problems associated with the expansion of the courts into ever more aspects of defendants' lives. Because drug court proponents come from within the criminal justice system, they are mindful of the procedural problems that can stem from, for example, a judge requiring a defendant to get birth control at Planned

Parenthood, or not allowing a defendant with a positive urine toxicology to see his or her child, or requiring a defendant to attend church or the ballet or a cultural event—all examples that advocates gave of court practice they thought verged into the "gray area" of bad drug court practice. Yet, uniformly, the advocates I spoke with, even when expressing concern, reverted to the entrenched nature of addiction to argue that the expanded jurisdiction of the court served to cure people's addictions. As one advocate explained:

> You end up crafting conditions as a judge. . . . You get into living arrangements. So you're going through drug treatment and your partner isn't. I mean, well, do you have any business saying who you can live with or that your partner has to accompany you to drug treatment? I mean, you get into areas that border, if they were really tested in a strict constructionist court . . . does the court have any business doing it? Would it be upheld on appeal? I suspect some of them, maybe a lot of them, wouldn't. . . . And I think you have to be cognizant of getting in areas that you don't belong. But you also have to be willing, with a court and in particular being a judge, to be a risk taker. What's necessary to make Susie Smith or Johnny Smith comply with the drug treatment protocols? Or to benefit . . . from drug treatment?

As another advocate explained:

> [Drug courts] are very focused on changing the litigants' behavior and in doing that become, the court becomes involved in participants' lives in a way that I think is potentially very dangerous. I've visited a lot of drug courts and I've seen things that I *do not* think are appropriate. They're overreaching. I've heard drug court judges talk to participants about who they're dating, who they're having sex with, how are they eating, where are they living, get an education, get a job. And it's very, very intrusive and I think that to some degree that's OK and is justified and on balance, it's appropriate, but I think it can go too far.

As someone else explained, "You've got what they call 'net widening.' People involved significantly in the criminal justice system in a way that they never would have been before. . . . If it's monitored carefully and there are things in place that provide checks and balances, that's OK. If they're not, then I think it's potentially dangerous from that perspective." As another person has warned:

> This is a profoundly slippery slope. How much can you legitimately require someone to achieve, and do the requirements need to be related to criminal involvement? I think we would all agree that a drug court can require clean urines and attendance at treatment because drug use is a crime. When you start requiring . . . other things . . . including a bank account, to what extent are you pushing the court beyond its natural jurisdiction? And how are you going to respond to the kinds of violations that will inevitably occur?[32]

Despite expressing this concern, most advocates thought that, in the end, the overstepping is worth it and justified because of the nature of addiction and the ensuing criminality. As one advocate explained:

> I think that drug courts need to be very careful about proportionality. . . . You've seen drug courts overextending themselves to saying to people you can't smoke cigarettes. You hear these kinds of stories. And one is not supportive of that. But having said that, I think there's a range of addicted offenders whose criminal behavior is such that courts can appropriately require them to do things other than require them to stay clean and sober. And so I think that . . . it's a case-by-case basis, what is and is not appropriate in terms of the severity of the person's behavior and the nature of their addiction.

Despite expressing reservations when asked, one proponent explained, summing up the general perspective of the people I interviewed, that "we're fighting a war against addiction. I hate to call it a war against drugs because it's not, it's really a battle against addiction," which is best fought with "the coercive power of the justice system." Therefore we should do "everything within our power" to fight this battle and "fix broken folks." Often, when discussing the court's overstepping, advocates would distance it from drug court overall, calling this type of court a "bad drug court." Or as one person said, "Just because something calls itself a drug court doesn't mean it is a drug court." The overwhelming consensus was that when courts do overstep, it's nothing inherent in the drug court model itself, rather a reflection of bad practice.

Defending drug courts against the charge of overstepping, one proponent, Greg Berman, has written:

> It is possible to find some examples of shoddy practice happening in drug
> courts across the country. It would be foolish not to admit this. It would
> be even more foolish to try and defend such practices. The truth is that
> any system staffed by idiosyncratic and fallible humans will occasionally
> result in bad practice. Bad practice should be rooted out of problem-solv-
> ing courts, just as it should be rooted out of conventional courts.[33]

But, Berman, goes on to argue:

> Put simply, there is no evidence to suggest that shoddy judging and sub-
> standard lawyering is any more widespread in drug courts than in conven-
> tional state courts. Quite the contrary. There is good reason to believe that
> these closely-watched experiments, with their emphasis on state-of-the-
> art technology, accountability and formalized systems of sanctions and
> rewards, actually reduce the potential for judges and other court players
> to run amok.[34]

"Enlightened Coercion"

In making their "case for coercion," drug courts emphasize the key role
that coercion plays in the therapeutic setting.[35] It is at the level of cure, at
the level of treatment, where drug courts make an intervention and make
coercion the key feature of that intervention. The attention advocates
play to sanctions and rewards, "the carrots and sticks," speaks to what the
courts can offer over jail or other forms of coerced treatment. By making
a strong argument in favor of coercion in treatment, however, they are essentially moving beyond criminality to weigh in on theories of addiction
more broadly.

While drug court advocates argue that coerced treatment is more humane than imprisoning addicts or subjecting them to the "revolving door
of justice," they also argue that coerced treatment is better than voluntary
treatment precisely because the court can enact the coercion necessary
to cure people's addictions. They build the necessity for coercion into the
ways they describe addiction and addicts. Because addiction is chronic

and relapsing, and because addicts don't want to be cured, coercion is best. They reorient the discussion away from the criminality of the *defendant* to the *client* or *participant* as addict, and thus have started focusing more on the disease than the action that led to someone's being under the supervision of the drug court in the first place.

Drug court advocates argue that "force is the best medicine." Sally Satel, a frequent editorial writer about drug courts, has written that "strict monitoring . . . is so often the best medicine for people with addictions."[36] When talking about the benefits of coercion, advocates move away from talking about criminals and branch out, broadly, to encompass theories of what works best with not only addicts, but also drug users. One person explained, "Voluntary treatment participation is wildly less successful than coerced treatment." Another summed up the role of coercion this way:

> Addicts by and large do not wake up one morning and go, "Hmm, I think I'm doing too many drugs and I'm going to go and get myself some treatment." And if they do that, they don't stay in treatment. . . . The coercion doesn't have to come from the court . . . but the court, the court obviously has its methods . . . a lot of the coercive power. . . . So I think it's nice the idea that you don't jail addicts. But you've got to do something. You can't just not jail them and think that's going to solve the problem.

As one drug treatment program director explained:

> The involvement of the court in treatment—especially in the use of their coercive power—has really benefited substance users. Before drug courts, treatment providers knew that clients were open to help when they were in crisis. . . . But as soon as they started feeling better, they'd leave. They'd say, "OK, I'm not sick now. The crisis is gone. I can leave treatment." Drug courts allow [treatment providers] to keep people in treatment long enough to break through the denial and to have good progress down the road.[37]

Advocates routinely cite the "evidence-based" approach that proves that addicts need coercion. They argue, almost consistently, that "the empirical data on drug treatment programs unequivocally . . . support[s] . . . this proposition"—that coercion is the key to rehabilitation. One article on drug courts explains that "treatment retention rates—a key indicator of long-term sobriety—are twice as high for participants in drug courts as opposed to individuals who seek out treatment voluntarily."[38] As another advocate explained:

> The top chronic offenders, chronic drug users, are very resistant to treatment. They have long-term patterned behavior that is very hard to break. Can you break that patterned behavior without any sort of coercive element? Well, the literature seems to suggest that the coercive part, that coercing treatment is more, at least as effective, if not more than voluntary treatment.

As another advocate put it, "It's true addicts could use their willpower. But they're not going to."

While advocates often cite the research showing that coerced drug treatment is better than voluntary treatment, they also appeal to what they view as common sense. As one person explained to me, "How many of us would floss our teeth better in the morning if the dentist stood over us? An addict . . . they need to be coerced." They further explained:

> It's about all of the different obstacles and barriers that get in the way of an addict making changes in their life. Just about the process of change. And that we can all, every one of us has had multiple failures at changing things in our own life. And to be able to help somebody wake up to the idea that change is tough. That even little things we try to change, whether it's trying to stop biting my fingernails, or try to stop cussing, or try to stop speeding, or spending too much money, whatever it is, it's not easy. Surely, we understand that that's a very difficult thing to do psychologically, sociologically.

This advocate is appealing to the "commonsense" idea that everyone has "bad habits" they want to change, and would most likely do so if they had some kind of authority holding them accountable. While this might be the case for some people, it's also true that if the consequence for continued speeding or nail chewing or shoe shopping were a weekend or more in jail, most people would balk at this method of behavior change. By focusing on the habit and not the force, this advocate attempts to make drug courts seem like a logical extension of the kinds of struggles everyone has with aspects of themselves they want to change. They are attempting to make coercion seem reasonable, especially to those of us who might never directly experience it in the ways all drug court defendants will.

Advocates are also mindful of critiques of coercion, but in general they do not view these as critical components of drug court practice they need to defend. As one advocate explained:

> You're in criminal justice. It is coercive. You are using coercion. This isn't voluntary. It is voluntary in the sense that you can choose to do this or go down the normal road and we can tell you what the normal road is. But this is all coercive. That's criminal justice. That's why it's different from not criminal justice. And so the question is, what's the appropriate role of coercion?

As another advocate explained:

> It's the left that is far more reluctant to buy into the drug courts.... They are theoretically opposed to the idea of using criminal sanctions as a means of punishing a disease. But the theory that we shouldn't coerce people with a disease to do anything . . . just puts principle ahead of pragmatism. And that becomes a theoretical debate. That's moral philosophy, that's not policy anymore. Moral philosophy tends to make lousy policy.

While this advocate views moral *philosophy* as counter to good public policy, morality is central to the idea and practice of coerced drug treatment. That drug court advocates don't view their work as a type of moral crusade speaks to the way addiction operates as a powerful social fact;[39] it is so accepted as problematic that any intervention meant to cure it is seen as pragmatic. The moral and theoretical underpinnings of drug court advocates' construction of addiction as a disease curable by force are rendered invisible in an approach that is seen as "common sense" rather than the accumulation of ideological perspectives that render habitual substance use and users suspect; their problematic relationship to drugs necessitates regular surveillance and coercion to bring them tentatively—because "relapse is inevitable"—back to law-abiding behavior and sobriety.

The anthropologist William Garriott has recently coined the term "narcopolitics" to describe the particular ways that concerns about threatening bodies are framed within the logic of illicit drug regulation.[40] Narcopolitics is a type of governance that uses illicit drugs for its justification and includes discourses, institutions, policy decisions, scientific statements, and moral propositions that stem from a concern with illicit drugs. This type of governance has come to dominate the legal system, where drug use is the rationale for much of the criminal justice system's actions. But narcopolitics is a manifestation of a broader "rhetoric of drugs"[41] that views a person's relationship to mind-altering substances as fundamental to their identity. This rhetoric is linked to practices that explicitly evoke psychological and medical theories of addiction as much as they call for law enforcement responses. Addicts who enter the criminal justice system, then, are governed by these different logics. Viewed as both sick and bad, these drug users are subject to disciplinary techniques, including rehabilitation and jail.

Addiction is a key area in which this individualistic approach takes place, particularly because compulsive substance use is conceptualized as a disease of the will as much as it has been conceptualized as a disease that has genetic origins and can be mapped in the brain.[42] Because of the simultaneous, and seemingly contradictory, emphasis on willpower and genetic predisposition to addiction, the disease model of addiction has never fully taken hold, providing room for the hybrid criminological, psychological, and medical model on which drug courts operate. The sociologist Nikolas Rose has argued that psychology is often in the service of governance, articulating who and how to govern and to what end.[43] This "government of the soul" is made possible through norms provided by psychology about what it means to be a healthy person. The concept of addiction becomes a tool for governing people and ensuring conformity toward the norm of sobriety—articulated by psychology and medicine—and the norm of law-abiding—provided by criminal justice. While these norms are expected of everyone, they are forced onto people who have proven unable to govern themselves accordingly.

Drug courts are, of course, unthinkable outside a discourse that casts habitual substance use as the disease of addiction, whose cure rests with the criminal justice system and courts specifically. Drug courts, because they are concerned with the future action of addicts, punish past actions as much as they govern the future behavior of addicts, justified in the language of the risk of relapse and the threat of future drug use.[44]

Drug courts emerge in an environment where scientific theories about the effects of drugs on the brain predominate, but in which addiction's manifestation is seen through behaviors considered to be associated with, or the outgrowth of, drug use. This model, then, is really a behavioral rather than medicalized approach to addiction, and leaves ample opportunity for the criminal justice system, with its focus on behavior, to assert a role for itself in recovery. The criminal justice system, with the help of treatment, teaches substance users about themselves as people who can be helped, through behavioral therapy, but who are always susceptible to their disease, despite this help.[45] It teaches them the value of responsibility and instills in them a dialectic of freedom and determination: they are sick with a disease whose cure rests in their willpower.[46] They are reminded of this willpower each time they are rewarded for abstinence or punished for their drug use.

Drug court advocates expand the boundaries of traditional criminal justice practice, overseeing increasing aspects of defendants' lives in the name of curing, or at least managing, defendants' addictions. They rely on the disease model to argue for enhanced judicial control of drug addicts and stake their claims on their supposed influence on the future behavior of defendants.

Advocates of coerced treatment see drug courts as an important part of both the "war on addiction" and of institutional reform within the criminal justice system. Drug court advocates are motivated both by the desire to keep addicts out of prison and by the desire to keep them under the supervision of the courts; and they have argued, in journal articles and editorials, strenuously against criminal justice reforms that seek to minimize the criminal justice system's control over illicit drug users or permit people to access treatment without judicial monitoring and oversight.[47] As one advocate explained, "Drug court is as close to decriminalization as we've gotten. . . . With decriminalization, we lose a very, very valuable ally in the war against addiction . . . and that is the coercive power of the justice system."

The goals of this coercion remain quite vague. The broad goals of drug courts, from abstinence to improved family relations to job stability, and their increased oversight of defendants, lead to two key consequences that are a direct outgrowth of a model that explicitly fuses rehabilitation and punishment. First, drug courts expand the scope of activities the courts monitor, in the name of helping people, and draw on prevailing theories of addiction and recovery to justify their expanded jurisdiction. This increased role seems inherent in a model that combines contradictory approaches to substance use—therapeutic, medical, and criminal—and does so under the control of such a powerful institution as the criminal justice system.

Second, drug courts are helping to transform prevailing notions about addiction by arguing that coercion is the key to getting people to stay in treatment long enough for it to be effective. The idea that the behaviors associated with drug use are amenable to change through coercion has received support from the leading institution on addiction in United States, the National Institute on Drug Abuse, which argues that "strong motivation [through institutions such as the criminal justice system] can facilitate the treatment process."[48]

Both of these consequences are a direct outgrowth of the logic of caring that guides drug court practitioners' activities, combined with their attempt to reform both how courts operate and the public's perception of courts as legitimate community-oriented institutions. Referred to as "good courts," problem-solving courts are an explicit attempt to use courts to address—and solve—entrenched social problems.[49] In this sense, they greatly resemble the "court-based regime[s] of social governance" of the Progressive Era.[50] Like these earlier courts, they draw on outside disciplinary perspectives to articulate an enhanced role for the court as an institution that uses its punitive power to coerce rehabilitation in the name of "helping" people. In doing so, the advocates of drug courts—and problem-solving courts more generally—reform how the criminal justice system understands and responds to drug-related offenses while firmly cementing the control of addiction in the hands of this same system.

6

"Now That We Know the Medicine Works"

Expanding the Drug Court Model

Now that we know the medicine works, we need to expand the system so that we can provide the medicine to everybody who needs it.
—James Milliken, San Diego County Judge

DRUG COURTS ARE interested in intervening at the level of the individual and, as demonstrated in the previous chapter, take considerable care to craft a therapeutic function for themselves, drawing on medicalized theories of addiction bolstered by psychological theories of behavior change. While advocates are interested in rehabilitating individuals, they are also interested in rehabilitating the court system. As discussed in chapter 3, institutional problems at the level of court functioning, defined by advocates as inefficiency and ineffectiveness, led to the formation of the first drug courts and continue to motivate proponents of these courts to argue for their expansion.

But drug court advocates have far grander goals and are interested in making their long-term mark on the criminal justice system. It is "a critical moment in the life of drug courts," and one that, not surprisingly for a movement so focused on articulating and advancing itself, has become the subject of much reflection by drug court advocates.[1] These concerns are reflected in the recent themes for the annual national drug court conference: "Taking Drug Courts to Scale" in 2007, "Healthy Families, Healing Communities" in 2008, and "Putting a Drug Court in Reach of Every American in Need" in 2010.

Drug court advocates are concerned with defining what "institutionalization" of drug courts means and what it would look like; in doing so they articulate the broader goals of drug courts that move far beyond rehabilitating offenders. Drug court advocates conceptualize what success for the "drug court field" means through their articulation of the institutional goals of drug courts, and their ideas about how a "grassroots" innovation can be incorporated into mainstream criminal justice practice. The expansion of the drug court model to other behavioral arenas considered to be motivated by addiction, including driving under the influence of alcohol and gambling, and other therapeutic interventions, including mental health, has important ramifications that move beyond an exclusive interest in drugs to a more generalized concept of addiction.

The ways that drug court advocates define institutionalization and the often-conflicting ideas they present about it are revealing of some of the historical trends that have characterized punishment innovations throughout the history of the criminal justice system. They also highlight the contradictions inherent in the way advocates talk about addiction, as a disease, and the best way to ensure its effective treatment through the criminal justice system.

Drug courts are predicated on an individualized approach to punishment that takes into account very personal and encompassing aspects of a defendant's life to ensure meaningfully tailored therapeutic interventions. This approach conflicts with the desire to "mainstream" this model into large, bureaucratic court systems. And yet this mainstreaming would signify validation of the drug court model. When panels, focus groups, or roundtables are convened to discuss the future of drug courts, the overwhelming majority of participants come from the criminal justice system, rarely drug treatment, even more rarely the medical establishment, and never people who identify themselves as advocates for drug users. For an innovation meant to take a therapeutic or rehabilitative approach to punishment, this absence speaks to the fact that drug courts are a criminal justice and not a therapeutic innovation. And yet advocates don't want these courts to lose their "therapeutic" function. They are mindful that when punishment and therapy meet, under the umbrella of a vast and explicitly coercive network, the uniqueness of drug courts could be challenged.

The National Association of Drug Court Professionals' chief executive has warned that "the rising toll of substance abuse and addiction is undeniable and poses the greatest threat to our domestic welfare."[2] These courts, in existence for over two decades, are no longer considered an innovation, and yet, as one advocate explained, the fact that drug courts are "still experimenting" poses a challenge to their continued existence. Further, he explained, "I think the drug court movement is facing a really key moment in its life course. . . . I'm not convinced you'll see drug courts on the scale you do today in five years."

Drug court advocates are mindful that they need to move beyond the small-scale, experimental approach they've been taking, and move to "the next step seeking not just to replicate pilot drug courts, but rather to test system-wide availability of new approaches to the problem of addiction."[3] What this system would look like is directly influenced by the institutional goals that advocates articulate for drug courts.

In every interview I conducted, advocates were clear that they were interested in changing the court system in ways that reflected a new respect for the therapeutic, or rehabilitative, goals of drug courts. For one advocate, success would entail moving drug courts "from pilot experiment to a permanent part of the judicial landscape." Moving to this next step has entailed much thought by advocates about how to retain the features of drug courts while moving them beyond their fairly limited scope.

While focused on rehabilitating offenders, drug court advocates are clear that they are attempting to change how the criminal justice system handles drug-related offenses. In a roundtable on the future of drug courts, hosted by the Center for Court Innovation, participants articulated goals for drug courts that included transforming the "culture of the courthouse," correctional practice, judicial curriculum, the attitudes of judges and attorneys, public opinion and media coverage, and the level of integration between the courts and treatment providers.[4] Most participants were clear that these kinds of changes could occur only if drug courts became "mainstreamed" or, as one advocate I spoke with explained, they are "move[d] . . . from pilot experiment to a permanent part of the judicial landscape wherever you are."

The challenge for advocates is to conceptualize how drug courts would go to "scale" or become mainstreamed, and what this might do to the efficacy and function of these courts. One advocate explained:

That's a tension that we're still playing with and we haven't resolved it. . . . I think we're interested in seeing both, at the risk of trying to have our cake and eat it too. . . . There's strong evidence to support the continued expansion of drug courts. And I think . . . the challenge . . . is we've moved past the initial cadre of true believers. There's clearly a need to ensure that drug courts are good drug courts. . . . How do you prevent [drug courts] from becoming bureaucratized? How do you keep them cutting-edge? How do you keep that sense of mission that I think has been crucial to their early success? Can you uncouple problem solving from court specialization? Does this stuff only work in a specialized context which brings with it certain advantages? Can you bring some elements of this approach and spread them throughout the court system?

As another advocate explained of the expansion of drug courts:

> You then get to an important crossroads. Are you going to institutionalize these, are they going to become more than just the weird court down the hallway where they clap and touch people and cry and laugh, or are you going to become part of the DNA of the court system? When you . . . build drug courts into the court system . . . it's very hard because you've got to then start setting minimum standards . . . best practices . . . some kind of performance measure to track whether it works. . . . It all feels very good but it's labor-intensive . . . and you've got to set up . . . some ways to set boundaries. However . . . it is extremely difficult because drug courts are strong if for no other reason than they rest on a community-strength model. So you have to be very careful in setting best practices not to end up with any kind of cookie-cutter approach, overly bureaucratizing the process.

The theme of bureaucratization as a negative outcome, as opposed to institutionalization as a positive one, was echoed by many of the people I interviewed and in the drug court literature as well. Bureaucratization implies a loss of innovation. As one advocate explained, "Does it have to lose its original aims? Or is that just normal? And then, well, what's the next wave that's coming after that?" One participant in the Center for Court Innovation's roundtable explained the distinction between bureaucratization and institutionalization this way: "Bureaucracy creates a coercive style of leadership that forces other people to act in a certain way. Institutionalization is a motivational style of leadership, which gets people inspired, and allows them to build their own teams and create programs with some flexibility."[5] The irony, of course, is that drug courts are explicitly coercive, with respect to defendants. But, as this proponent's viewpoints reflects, some drug court leaders and staff want the freedom to design courts with the flexibility to make this coercion an inspirational practice for those who are enforcing it.

Yet it is precisely this flexibility that some drug court advocates believe needed to be curtailed if drug courts increased in size and scope. Some advocates spoke of the need for "best practices" if more judges are going to be involved in drug court–style practice. As one advocate explained, it is the "charismatic leadership" aspect of drug courts that could lead to their demise "because it's so informal and because it is do whatever you want," which will be "daunting to get anyone to fill courts as judges turn over" unless some "demystification of the process" takes place.

The advocates I spoke with were unclear about how this demystification would take place. The recent literature on drug courts and institutionalization, much of it written by drug court researchers, has started to mention the need for a court "accreditation" system as an attempt to standardize drug court practice across jurisdictions. Doug Marlowe, who has conducted extensive research studies on drug courts, argued that "the responsibility now falls to the drug-court field to establish performance benchmarks and best practices for drug-court programs and to develop accreditation procedures that can be used to document whether a particular program is in compliance with professionally accepted standards of practice."[6] Others argue that "the ultimate goal is to institutionalize drug courts, and standardization of performance measurement will assist in this effort. Standardized measures and indicators will provide policymakers and other stakeholders with information to continue support and sustenance for the movement."[7] Arguing for the benefits of accreditation, the Urban Institute's John Roman wrote, "A more formalized research process funneled through an objective accreditation process, best practices and future advances can be institutionalized. Accreditation will allow drug courts to evolve and to innovate while at the same time taking them out of the self-promotion business."[8]

While a few people have argued for accreditation with an objective agency designating drug courts as such, others see the success of drug courts as their ultimate demise. As a roundtable participant explained, "I would like to see every court in my state thinking of itself as a substance abuse court, and operating with that kind of consciousness about these issues."[9] Another said, "I share the vision of making this a way of doing business across the justice system, and maybe even fading drug courts out of existence as their tenets become embedded in practice."[10]

But, as some of the advocates I spoke with pointed out, if all courts engaged in drug-court style practices, it would be impossible to coordinate services and engage with defendants in a deep and personalized way. As one advocate explained:

> Is bigger better? I don't know the answer to that. . . . There are these big, what we call drug court systems, where they take everybody... everyone that smells like a drug-using offender is assessed and they go to different tracks. I got to tell you, they're giving up a lot of the tenets. . . . But also I think that, as a general reform, that as a general institutionalization, to see every judge be therapeutic, to see the value of treatment, to at least make an initial decision, let's get this person assessed to see what the problem is, I think that that goes a long way to reforming how we do business in the courts with addicts and anybody that has a problem that's emerging in courts.

A minority of the advocates I spoke with expressed concern about the potential reversion to explicit punitiveness that could accompany the institutionalization of drug courts. One person asked, "At some point does it get too big where you're just doing the same thing, you're just disposing of cases, and not giving people the attention, and you're not using the science? I just don't know." As another person explained:

> That's my worry about drug courts, judges got discretion back and they got able to jail people now fairly freely like the good old days: "Yeah, you're going to jail." So they like it. Well, if you're talking about a balanced number of responses to various kinds of behaviors, one of them over here is confinement. . . . But it was never the main thing. It was all about *not* doing that. And the longer in [treatment], the more success, is the most self-serving industry truism that there is.

Another advocate explained that, with institutionalization, drug courts lose important oversight that helps to temper their action. In the face of diminished oversight, "Drug courts constantly battle slipping back into that punitive place . . . we came from. . . . It's a hell of a lot better than the traditional system, I promise you that, but there are tendencies to go back to that punitive state which we're trying to reform." Or as one drug court advocate warned:

> To me the inescapably historical analogy is the juvenile court movement, which succeeded spectacularly in going to scale. . . . The most prominent

problem with juvenile courts—as they became widespread and institutionalized—was the lack of due process, poor fact finding, indefinite jurisdiction over people based on a small offense, and idiosyncratic judging.
It was a lawless court. As we develop drug courts, we need to keep this
experience in mind.[11]

This advocate expressed a viewpoint that was in a decided minority,
in both the drug court literature and among the people I interviewed.
Drug court proponents truly believe that this model represents progress and consider its adoption by the criminal justice system the next
step. While they debate what this adoption would look like—more specialized drug courts, or more therapeutic practice on the part of judges
across courts—they are firmly convinced that coerced treatment is the
right response for addressing the problems of repeated drug-related
offenders.

Drug court advocates rest this conviction on the disease model of addiction; this gives them the leverage to make the case for coerced treatment within the courts. Anthony Platt, in his book on the rise of the juvenile courts and the invention of delinquency in the Progressive Era in
the United States, explained that imagery of crime at the time was heavily
influenced by "the acceptance of the medical model and the 'rehabilitative
ideal.'"[12] This medical model influenced a transformation in crime control
policies, "from one emphasizing the criminal nature of delinquency to the
'new humanism,' which speaks of disease, illness, contagion and the like.
The emergence of the medical warrant is of considerable significance, since
it is a powerful rationale for organizing social action in the most diverse
behavioral aspects of our society."[13]

As I have shown, drug court advocates used medicalized theories of
addiction to argue for increased court oversight into multiple aspects
of defendants' lives to sufficiently intervene in the complex condition
of addiction. While they may conceptualize addiction as an illness with
biological origins and clinical indicators, both rooted in the brain, drug
court advocates merge the medical and behavioral theories around addiction and recovery to articulate a strong role for the courts in the lives
of defendants. As Platt showed, Progressive Era courts did the same thing
over one hundred years ago, and as many of the writers on Progressive
Era court reform in the United States have demonstrated, this increased
oversight left ample room for the kind of court expansion—"indefinite

jurisdiction" and "idiosyncratic judging"—that the advocate quoted above warned about.

Expanding the Drug Court Model

Through their reliance on individualizing perspectives, drug court advocates help to create a new type of addict. The addict they construct is both sick and bad. The drug court addict is sick with a brain disease, and yet the addict's recovery depends on court-monitored drug treatment, coercion, and even intermittent time in jail, in this instance justified as a "treatment tool" rather than punishment. In order to construct drug courts and the criminal justice system as the place to provide treatment, drug court advocates create an addiction that is complex in its nature, in both its origins and the way it manifests itself, and in what it takes to eradicate, or at least temper, this addiction. By justifying the logic and practice of drug courts, advocates not only draw on medicalized theories of addiction that originate outside the criminal justice system, they also contribute to these theories by arguing for the important link between coercion and recovery. Drug court advocates draw on prevailing theories of addiction and recovery to make their intervention. By merging these theories to the specific practice of court-mandated, judicially monitored treatment, these advocates help construct new theories about addiction, recovery, addicts, criminals, and the criminal justice system.

Drug court advocates genuinely believe that what they are doing is a radical departure and that their efforts at rehabilitation differ from previous generations' with the explicit "responsibility" that is laid on the defendants to be active participants in their own cure. They enter into debates over punishment by positing that people transgress norms because they are sick, but that their cure requires an institutional intervention that heavily relies on the court, combined with the individual motivation of defendants to stop using drugs. Drug courts, then, are guided by the dual belief that people can enact changes in their behavior *and* that their behavior is motivated by some outlying factor not entirely within their control. This duality is at the heart of rehabilitative sanctions.

Drug courts are rehabilitative; people are mandated to drug treatment and therapeutic sanctions. These courts are also punitive; defendants who fail at treatment are punished, often with jail sentences or other sanctions

that are meant to enact some kind of psychic pain. Drug court "participants" are considered sick with a brain disorder whose cure is most amenable to court-supervised, judicially led treatment. And ultimately, because they suffer from a "chronic, relapsing condition," addicts can never
be cured. But, advocates argue, the chances of addicts remaining abstinent
from drugs are enhanced the longer they stay in treatment, and people
stay in treatment longer when coerced. According to this logic, coerced
treatment is not only expedient, it is the preferred way to deal with addiction. It is through this logic that drug court advocates make their "case for
coercion."

This idea that coerced behavioral sanctions can be an effective way to
deal with "sick" criminal offenders is expanding horizontally, to different disease categories, and vertically to different age groups. Judges now
preside over gambling courts, drunk-driving courts, homelessness courts,
and mental health courts, all areas where defendants are mandated to
treatment and intensive supervision. All these courts are premised on the
idea that treatment and punishment work when applied together. They
are predicated on the idea that a personalized approach, combined in the
unifying force of the criminal justice system, can cure the ills that produce
criminality.

"Expanding the Medicine"

While the expansion of drug courts can be considered a sign of their success, perhaps their most important triumph is an ideological one. They
have helped herald in the idea that that criminality can be motivated by a
form of badness and sickness that it is the court's responsibility to work on
as both a punitive and a therapeutic agent. Mental health courts, stemming
directly from the drug court model, are similarly based on the premise
that defendants are sick with a disease that plays a significant part in their
criminal behavior. A primer on mental health courts explains that mental
illness is a "genuine neurobiological disease of the brain," and that "the
functioning of the brain is essentially outside the direct control of the individual."[14] Despite the fact that the disease is outside of one's control, these
courts rely on a system of sanctions and rewards based on the assumption
that individuals can and will control their behavior in response to specific
stimuli. Currently, there are approximately 175 mental health courts in

operation, up from four in 1997 and seventy in 2004. Their expansion has been made possible by the Law Enforcement and Mental Health Project, an act passed by the U.S. Congress in 2000 meant to address the needs of people with mental illness in the criminal justice system.

Mental health courts monitor defendants' drug use but, unlike drug courts, they are testing for compliance with drug regimens as well as ingestion of illicit substances. As a manual outlining the essential elements of these courts explains, "The court must have up-to-date information on whether participants are taking medications, attending treatment sessions, abstaining from drugs and alcohol, and adhering to other supervised conditions."[15] The use of pharmaceuticals, mandated as treatment, complicates the court's surveillance; some drugs framed as *medication* are permitted, and even required, while others, framed as *drugs and alcohol*, are seen as counter to the defendant's progress in court. Again, as with drug courts, these courts are based on the idea that sanctions and incentives, punishment and rewards, are the best way to treat the biologically rooted disorder of mental illness.

While this view of criminality as a form of illness has expanded to mental health via the drug court model, it is also expanding into other aspects of life that are framed within the lens of addiction. Two such courts, DWI/DUI and gambling court, are both premised on the idea that the defendant has an addiction that is best treated through coercion. DWI/DUI courts are similar to drug courts with the exception that all of them are based on a post-conviction model. There are currently 526 such courts in the United States. Unlike drug courts, DWI/DUI courts rely extensively on "community supervision" as a way of monitoring defendants' compliance with treatment. As the National Drug Court Institute explains, this supervision is an important way "to monitor participant's behavior outside the courtroom. . . . It is imperative that your whole team is aware of what the participant is doing in the community."[16] This extensive supervision is considered essential as a way to monitor compliance with treatment. Additionally, DWI/DUI courts utilize surveillance technologies such as the Secure Continuous Remote Alcohol Monitoring System (SCRAM, often called "electronic tethers"), ankle devices put on defendants that can detect alcohol use from perspiration tests conducted every half hour. According to their manufacturer, Alcohol Monitor Systems,[17] SCRAMs are used to monitor more than 150,000 people in almost every state in the country. Gambling courts, much more in their infancy, are described by the National Drug Court Institute as serving "those suffering from a pathological or compulsive gambling disorder."

Explicitly modeled after drug courts, they are attempting to reframe gambling as a "psychological disorder" rather than a "character flaw."[18] Unlike drug and drunk driving courts, they cannot regularly "test" for the presence of gambling, so they also face a surveillance challenge as well. Despite this, many states (including those with legalized gambling) are considering starting these courts, modeling them on drug courts.

Juvenile Drug Courts

Juvenile drug courts bear the most similarity to adult drug courts, both in their operation but also in the connections they posit between addiction and the loss of volition. Unlike adult drug courts, juvenile ones are operated under a dual notion of dependency. Youth are addicts, dependent on drugs, but they are also young, and therefore especially dependent on their families, legal guardians, and, most important, the courts. While drug court proponents argue that addicts are "like children," a negative assessment that characterizes an inability to think about the consequences of one's actions, youth vulnerability and propensity toward deviance is explicitly evoked in the rationale for juvenile drug courts as part of their strategy to cure juvenile offenders. Like adult drug courts, juvenile drug courts rely on and contribute to ideas of what addiction is; in this instance, they help *create* the idea of the "adolescent addict" as a particular, and distinct, type of deviant. Because they can highlight the "youth" part as much as, if not more than, the addict part, expanded oversight of the family become paramount; families or legal guardians are viewed as both a key to youths' "recovery" as well as a possible source of their continued addiction.

Young people are also coming under increasing scrutiny with coerced rehabilitative sanctions such as juvenile drug courts. Over 50% of youth in publicly funded drug treatment are mandated there through the criminal justice system, a percentage that increases yearly and has almost doubled over the past ten years.[19] The first official juvenile drug courts opened in 1986. Like adult drug courts, young people receive intensive supervision from the judge and court staff while under the purview of the courts and drug treatment. The goal of these courts is to "correct and rehabilitate children who violated the law, to protect the community from their delinquent behavior, and to strengthen the family."[20]

The sociologist Leslie Paik, in her ethnography of a Southern California juvenile drug court, explains that "the focus of juvenile drug court, then, is about not only regulating drug use but also reshaping these youths into more responsible citizens who engage in positive activities."[21] These courts are actively constructing what it means to be "responsible" through their subtle and overt corrections of young people for things that aren't necessarily illegal but are considered inappropriate for youth. Children should go to school, be respectful to parents and guardians, and not stay out late; youth in juvenile drug courts face legal ramifications for breaking rules such as these in a process where "otherwise normal behaviors" are made illegal. Paik noted custodial "remedies" (meaning punishments) for these infractions that ranged from shorter stints in juvenile hall to longer stays in probation camp. Youth could be punished for having a "bad attitude" in relation to the court, schools, and treatment. Much like adult drug courts, youth are evaluated based on a range of behaviors not considered illegal but framed as crucial to the recovery process.

Juvenile drug courts, then, construct the good youth; much like their Progressive Era counterpart courts, they contribute to the construction of youth as they draw on prevailing assumptions of young people as dependent and in need of guidance from adults. While they are focused on coercing "normal" youth behavior, they are also focused on drug use and, like adults drug courts, regularly drug test defendants. As Paik explains, these courts are "a surveillance mechanism designed as treatment," with drug tests as one part of this system of monitoring.[22]

But, as Paik also notes, drug court staff engage in a lot of "interpretive work" around these drug tests, which provide an "uncertain verdict" when combined with the staff's assumptions about the particular youth being monitored. Negative drug tests, a seemingly objective marker of abstinence, could be used to justify increased drug testing for problem youth, with the assumption that the initial drug tests failed and more monitoring would root out noncompliance. The assumption was that some youth are, by their nature, liars, and the court's job was to change this aspect of their deviance (among many others).

That these courts are dealing with "youth" means that they emphasize and require the participation of young people's families in the court processing. In juvenile drug courts, a greater emphasis is placed:

on the role of the family in all facets of court operations, from assessment and treatment, to courtroom procedures, to the structure of rewards and sanctions. Juvenile drug courts usually include more significant outreach to each offender's home and community. They are more likely to mobilize the efforts of other significant people in the youths' lives to create teams of program partners that can teach, supervise, coach and discipline youthful offenders.[23]

The language used to describe these courts is very important: they are meant not only to *punish* young offenders but to supervise, discipline, and coach them toward law-abiding adulthood. Part of this emphasis on family has to do with these courts' theories of juvenile drug use that reflect the emerging "science" as depicted by the National Institute on Drug Abuse. As Nora Volkow, MD, the head of NIDA, has recently explained, "The adolescent brain is different from that of an adult. And that leads to behavior that definitely puts them at much higher risk to want to try drugs than the brain of an adult." Because youth are at greater risk for *wanting to try drugs* and "have even less override of their impulsivity," it is "much more important to overreact possibly."

This call to "overreact" is bolstered by the recent trend to use biological studies of teen substance use to set their susceptibility apart from that of adults; these studies are being used to create a new type of addict. A recent study about cocaine-seeking behavior of "adolescent" and adult rats found that adolescent rats "show delayed extinction of drug seeking compared to adults" when exposed to cocaine.[24] This finding has been interpreted by Join Together, a now-defunct informational site about drug policy, prevention, and treatment that was sponsored by Boston University's School of Public Health, to "hint at greater teen susceptibility to addiction."[25] The website BiologyNews.net, echoing Join Together's interpretation of the study's findings, explains that "evidence that younger brains get stuck on drug-related stimuli reinforces real-world data. Epidemiological studies confirm that of people in various age groups who experiment with drugs, teens are by far the most likely to become addicted."[26]

In juvenile drug courts, families are implicated in addiction's causes and cure in more complex ways; they are seen as a potential source of help for drug use but also as a potential hindrance to recovery and the source of the addiction in the first place. The goals of these courts are to "counteract the negative influences of peers, gangs and family members."[27] The social networks of the youth under supervision are directly implicated in their disease; we are told that they often come from "families with substance abuse problems, some of which have gone on for generations."[28] For this reason, these courts have "a much greater focus on the functioning of the family" than do traditional drug courts and standard criminal justice processing. These courts provide "intensive judicial intervention and supervision of juveniles and families involved in substance abuse—a level of intervention not generally available through the traditional juvenile court process."[29] Because youth, unlike adults, are living with their families, "the juvenile drug court must shift its focus from a single participant to the entire family," and include the family in the youth's recovery process.[30] This can be difficult, however, because "disenfranchised families often face overwhelming problems, such as poverty, substance abuse, and lack of opportunity." It becomes the court's responsibility to engender trust in these families, to "build their confidence" and "empower them in their efforts to change."[31]

Part of this empowerment involves requiring a parent to attend and participate in court hearings. This can allow the judge and other court staff to see the child's interaction with his or her parents and "learn more about the problems and issues in the youth's life" that might stem from this interaction. While the parents are framed as crucial to the juvenile's recovery, it is also their relationship with the child that is part of the problem and thus relevant to the courts. As the Bureau of Justice Assistance primer on drug courts explains, "While gentle encouragement is the best way to involve a parent, be willing to enforce participation—even by initiating contempt procedures against parents who fail to participate. Occasionally, it may be necessary to order substance abuse evaluation and/or treatment for the parent."[32] At the same time the court is trying to overcome potential skepticism on the parents' part about the court's involvement in their lives, they can use this involvement in potentially punitive way. The treatment, then, becomes about correcting not only the young person's behavior but the behavior of adults as well.

The staff of juvenile drug courts are attentive to parents and the role they play in reporting "noncompliance" and enforcing "accountability." Paik describes in detail the relationship that occurs between parents or legal guardians and the drug court staff. One of Paik's most significant findings overall is that court staff are constantly constructing the ideas of noncompliance and accountability, often through their interpretation of seemingly "objective" data. Part of this data involves their analysis of parents or legal guardians, whom the courts view as their "eyes and ears," helping to serve as an additional layer of supervision and surveillance of youth. As one parent Paik interviewed explained, "This probation is not only his but mine. It has really affected me because it is like living, but not freely. . . . It is a lot of stress."[33] Paik found that the drug court staff categorized parents based on their willingness to work with the court. Good parents understood the importance of "accountability" and "compliance" and were willing to tell the court if their children broke rules. In contrast, uncooperative parents covered up their children's infractions and resented the court's intervention in their lives. The court would require some parents to attend drug treatment with their children if they seemed uncooperative or uninvolved.

Because families are sometimes viewed as a hindrance to their child's recovery in juvenile drug courts, the judge is framed as an important figure in the young person's life, "providing the structure and support that are otherwise absent. *In loco parentis* has a special meaning in this context."[34] The court monitors young people while simultaneously trying to establish trust. The information obtained while trying to establish this "trust" allows the court to devise rewards and punishments that "correspond directly to the youth's perception of a reward or consequence."[35]

One of the challenges for juvenile drug courts is how to graft theories of addiction developed for adults onto young people. The juvenile drug court primer explains that substance abuse "is referred to broadly as youth involvement with alcohol and other drugs (AOD) at all problem levels" but avoids explaining what "problem level" means.[36] Further, the authors explain, young people are "seldom addicted to alcohol and other drugs in the traditional sense, and they use alcohol and other drugs for reasons vastly different from those of adults."[37] As the primer further explains, "Most adolescent AOD use has not progressed to addiction and the AOD use is often associated with other risky behavior."[38] So, not only are young people not addicted like adults, they are potentially not addicted at all. Yet, despite this lack of addiction to drugs or alcohol, they are required to remain abstinent from drugs. Juvenile drug courts teach young people how to lead "productive and substance-free and crime-free lives."[39] These courts most directly hark back to the juvenile courts of the Progressive Era, where courts became the vehicles for disciplining unruly lower-class youth. Juvenile drug courts are based on an ideology of care that facilitates increased supervision of young people and their families, their schools, and their peers, in ways that traditional court processing prevents. As with adult drug courts, this is done in the name of caring and concern for the future of drug users. The judge becomes parent to both adults and juveniles in the system, coercing them toward recovery with both care for their addiction backed by the force of the criminal justice system.

The expansion of the drug court model speaks to the extent to which they tap into a faith in the power of the courts to both heal and punish, and in an enduring idea that "tough love" is the way to cure the badness and sickness of behavioral nonconformity. The criminal justice system, because of its dominance, can incorporate opposing views of criminality—as a willful form of rulebreaking or a disease-induced compulsion—and still retain control over how society responds to these infractions.

Drug and problem-solving court advocates generally view these reforms as alternatives to incarceration. This view is supported by the positive media coverage that depicts the problem not in terms of an expansive system of punishment that has brought considerably more people into its purview over the twentieth and into the twenty-first century, but as a managerial one: what should be done with rulebreakers once we apprehend them? Because of this view, that the problem is *how* to punish not *that* we punish so extensively, the solutions put forth to address the ineffective and costly incarceration crisis are cast as alternatives. Yet, when we view diffuse and concentrated forms of punishment as part of the same mechanism, we can see how the spread of drug court and other rehabilitative sanctions requires little ideological shift and is, in fact, compatible with the cultural preoccupation with getting punishment right.[40]

Michel Foucault, in his groundbreaking book *Discipline and Punish: The Birth of the Prison*, focused much of his work on the institutionalized, enclosed, and increasingly private modes of punishment, such as prison, schools, and factories, that emerged in the nineteenth century. In these enclosed spaces, he argued, surveillance was facilitated by the "panopticon," through which inmates could be observed at all times.[41] Foucault described prison as a system of surveillance and discipline. The "juridical subject," Foucault wrote, is "the obedient subject, the individual subject to habits, rules, orders, an authority that is exercised continually around him and upon him and which he must allow to function automatically on him."[42] Authorities enact this control and transformation of behavior by "the development of the knowledge of the individual"—behavioral and social sciences provide the rationale for punishment that is meant to be both punitive and transformative.

Because Foucault focuses his analysis on the type of surveillance and discipline enacted in prisons, other scholars have attempted to use his work to explain how discipline works in noninstitutional settings. This has led to a reformulation of Foucault's ideas to explain this movement from discipline that relies on and is enacted in closed spaces, to one that is more diffuse. Gilles Deleuze has written that we now have a "society of control" rather than Foucault's "disciplinary societies."[43] Deleuze argues that "institutions are finished. . . . Man is no longer man enclosed, but man in debt." Echoing this line of reasoning, scholars such as Deborah Lupton and Nikolas Rose have argued that, in essence, people no longer need to be controlled via the force of institutional structures; we have so thoroughly adopted the language and logic of control that force is not necessary.[44] In other words, we discipline our bodies (through diet and exercise) and our souls (via therapy, self-help, and treatment) willingly because this is what "good" people do; we enact on ourselves the discipline that used to be the state's purview.

And yet the United States has not reduced its reliance on prisons, probation, and parole; it incarcerates a larger percentage of its population than any other nation, with drug arrests largely fueling the continued expansion of the criminal justice system. Coerced sanctions such as drug courts use explicit force, and occasionally the enclosed structure of jails, to force behavior change on certain people—the ones most likely to encounter the criminal justice system in the first place. Racial bias permeates the criminal justice system, with African Americans far more likely than whites to be policed, arrested, charged, convicted, and sentenced for crimes. This is especially true with the policies associated with the War on Drugs where, despite national studies showing that the majority of illegal drug users are white, African Americans and Latinos are far more likely to be arrested for using illegal drugs.[45]

The increasing size and scope of the criminal justice system accompanied by the increasing medicalization of human life suggest that there are two parallel processes at play that are about both *discipline* and *control*. We seek both the biological and genetic basis of addiction while simultaneously arresting a greater number of drug users, many of whom we force into a tenuous sobriety. As drug court proponents discuss the fate of these courts and their model expands to ever more arenas of human life, this contradiction between free will and compulsion, criminality and disease, will be increasingly overcome as hybrid models, steeped largely in moral models of rulebreaking, proliferate.

Conclusion

In the end, when conscience and convenience met, convenience won. When treatment and coercion met, coercion won.
> —David Rothman, *Conscience and Convenience*

We need to be extremely careful about the kind of policies and interventions that we may wish to make in pursuit of the "civilized life."
> —Scott Vrecko, "'Civilizing Technologies' and the Control of Deviance"

ON JANUARY 5, 2010, the Internet buzzed with the story of Redmond O'Neal's drug relapse. O'Neal, famous for being the son of actors Ryan O'Neal and Farrah Fawcett, was arrested in February 2008 for driving under the influence and felony drug possession and was eventually sentenced to drug court after pleading guilty to his offenses. When he returned from a twenty-four-hour pass to his residential drug treatment program where he was serving his sentence, O'Neal admitted to and tested positively for drug use. He was sent back to court, where his judge admonished him: "You haven't got a clue as to what recovery means. . . . It's a lifetime commitment. It's grinding, hard, painful work." O'Neal was ordered to prison as punishment for his drug use, as a reminder that recovery is hard work—but also as a reminder that drug courts don't coddle addicts. Force and medicine go hand in hand, but when medicine fails, force is the best response.

O'Neal's relapse was immediately covered by celebrity gossip blogs. Perez Hilton, one of the most widely read gossip bloggers, with an estimated ten million different visitors a month, wrote, "Redmond is facing up to six years in prison now with his latest shenanigans violating his probation. He had been clean for six months. Sad, sad."[1] Readers of Hilton's blog immediately posted comments on this story; their support for O'Neal was mixed. "Send his sorry ass to jail—it's obvious rehab isn't working for him," Lucas wrote. "Time in prison may be what he needs to understand what reality really is," 2201East chimed in. Other posters were more sympathetic, referring to the "struggle" of addiction, the difficulty of fighting this "disease" publicly. "Ultimately clean time means so little . . . unless you truly embrace change in your life. . . . We addicts/alcoholics are adept liars," apo76 wrote, and askcherlock explained, "This guy has a disease. It's called addiction and there's no easy cure. He will fall, but hopefully one day he will be clean." Responding to a *Los Angeles Times* story on O'Neal's return to prison, reader Patricia wrote, "If jail is really good for drug addicts, then shouldn't we be offering this same benefit to relapsing alcoholics?"

Drug courts tap into prevailing cultural ideas about addiction, recovery, treatment and force, and the value of sobriety and self-control. These ideas are supported and reiterated by judges and doctors as well as celebrity gossip blog readers, by treatment providers and probation officers, friends and family, in newspapers, movies, music, and television shows, medical journals, and policy reports. These ideas are reflected in our seemingly very personal ideas about addiction, ideas derived from our experiences. And yet these ideas are reiterated and reinforced every time we read stories about addiction, watch documentaries that tell us that compulsive substance use is a disease and a brain disorder, or see feature films and reality television shows where addicts struggle. Addiction ruins lives, families, neighborhoods, communities. Sobriety is the only cure for this deadly disease. Abstinence is difficult to achieve, a daily struggle, and yet engaging in this struggle is the only way to get sober. Treatment is the only way to get clean. And, often, coerced treatment is the best route for addicts, helping them achieve a sobriety that would be impossible on their own. This is the kindest thing we can do for addicts, force them to face their demons and their drug use. Our current presidential administration agrees. Force truly is the best medicine.

Or is it? In this conclusion, I argue that force is not the best medicine. The marriage of punishment and treatment is a failed one; it's time for a divorce. This marriage did not work in the Progressive Era, it does not work now, and it will not work in the future. It will never work to eradicate habitual substance use because that is not its underlying goal. It is a tenuous success at managing unruly bodies, an add-on to the prison–industrial complex, but as a "revolutionary" strategy to the problems of crime and drugs, it comes nowhere close to addressing the problem. I argue that we need to reframe the problem not as the link between drugs and crime,[2] but rather our ideas about habitual substance use, the ideologies about addiction that we cling to despite the harm it causes drug users, its societal costs, and the impossibility of achieving a drug-free world. The problem might be the all-encompassing nature of the criminal justice system and the damage it causes people caught in its web. Seen in this light, then, asking the system that has created a problem to fix it only perpetuates the problem, and does little to affect the underlying ideologies that frame drug use as badness and sickness and that gives the powerful institution of criminal justice the last word as to whether and when someone is healed.

Unlike most works critical of the criminal justice approach to drugs, I am not going to conclude by heralding "treatment" as the solution to mass incarceration. Rather, I argue, it is this blind faith in treatment as the answer to the drug problem that is actually part of the problem, creating and perpetuating the idea that habitual substance users need to be fixed (in costly and often ineffective ways). Real alternatives to the criminalization and control of drug users require a radical reorientation in the way we conceptualize habitual substance users and the value we place on sobriety. The contradictory ways we deploy the words disease, medicine, health, and drugs reflect our confused distinctions between "good" drugs and "bad" drugs that get grafted onto drug users, some of whom are encouraged by the medical establishment to use drugs to cure a disease while others are encouraged by the criminal justice system to stop using drugs to cure a disease. Unless we confront our fraught cultural attitudes toward drugs and drug users, we will perpetuate a system of inequality where some drug users have their entire lives managed by a system with the power and mandate to punish.

Addiction as Disease

There is no evidence that habitual substance use is a disease, and yet this is the common "enlightened" understanding. As I showed in chapter 4, the disease model is a historical triumph but not an empirical one. We cannot locate addiction as a disease in the body and we cannot find the disease of addiction in the brain. We can see the effects, both positive and negative, of drug use on the body. We do know that drug use alters brain chemistry, as does every other activity in which humans engage. Habitual substance use, called addiction, is no more a disease than it is a failure of will; genetic predispositions or environmental factors don't make one sick with this disease. Habitual substance use is a varied phenomenon that we try to contain within our existing ideological paradigms that simultaneously value medicine and punishment. But, if we move between these two poles, both articulating a viewpoint that values sobriety, we stay within the paradigm that frames habitual substance use as a problem that must be controlled—and the way to control it is to stop it.

As a one-time advocate of the disease model of addiction, I understand that it is an attempt to put addiction in the hands of the medical establishment, undermining punitive approaches to substance users. But, as the historical record shows, these two perspectives have merged in important ways. Medical paradigms have not lessened punitive control of drug users. Medicine and criminal justice are distinct yet related systems of social control. Medicine, by staking its own claim on addiction, helps to retain the institutional control of drug users and, perhaps inadvertently, provides the justification for coerced treatment. Sick people need treatment. Sometimes sick people resist treatment. But if they are sick, they must be cured, for their and the community's sake, and force is one way to cure them. Additionally, the union between medicine and the criminal justice system is not a marriage between equals; when medicine and force combine, force overtakes medicine. When a defendant shows up in drug court repeatedly with "dirty urines," he or she will eventually be thrown in jail. The medicine hasn't worked, but force will.

Abstinence as Cure

The second major assumption guiding our views on drug use is that abstinence is the only cure for the disease of addiction. Addicts relapse but continued drug use of any amount and for any duration is considered a slip-up, a failure, a recurrence of the disease. Controlled drug use is not a possibility. And yet the evidence shows us that people like to use drugs and will continue to do so. They use drugs sometimes in dangerous ways, but often people control their drug use to maximize pleasure and minimize harm.[3] Even though people derive pleasure from drug use, we rarely talk about the pleasures associated with certain drug use, only the pain it causes.[4]

Allied with our view that substance use is a symptom of the disease of addiction is the idea that drug use is synonymous with pain. Drug use is about pain and suffering, pathology and compulsion. Scholars have recently begun to examine the absence of the discourse of pleasure in our dominant perspectives on substance use; in fact, the *International Journal of Drug Policy* recently devoted an entire issue to pleasure and drugs.[5] Pleasure as a motive for substance use is silenced as the substance use becomes a problem for the state, which is called on to govern this substance use. Problematic drug use is that which is without reason and compulsive; it is characterized by pain not pleasure. Within this framework, drug use is considered either a form of "beastliness," which requires force to stop, or a form of compulsion, which requires treatment. With drug courts, both of these are applied to stop drug users; it is inconceivable that their drug use brings them pleasure. This drug use is always linked to trauma and damage, at the level of the individual, family, and society. Pleasure as a warrantable motive for drug use is acceptable when this use is linked to social privilege; it is erased as the drug users under discussion become "problems." Their drug use is constructed as undesirable; it is linked to social ills such as crime, called a disease best treated with coercion. It is untenable, as our dominant ideology now holds, to imagine that drugs can cause both pleasure and pain for the same person. And it is even harder to accept that the pain associated with drug use is caused, or at least exacerbated by, the state response that demands we "do something" about this drug use.

Our faith in sobriety as the cure for the disease of addiction has caused much harm, far more than drug use has caused. People are ostracized and jailed based on this faith. In the United States, people with drug-related felony convictions lose their housing, jobs, social services, and access to their children.[6] They are made into social pariahs in a process that has continued since the emergence of the medical model of addiction over two hundred years ago. And yet two hundred years have shown us that people will continue to use drugs despite these negative consequences. The reasons they continue to do so are less important than the fact that it happens.

Sound drug policy must take into account that people derive pleasure from drugs. We rarely hear about this pleasure because we rarely hear from habitual substance users when it comes time to discuss, debate, and develop drug policy. Physicians, judges, lawyers, psychologists, and sociologists, to name a few, tell us what it means to be a habitual substance user; they tell us what addicts need. As I showed in chapter 5, drug courts proponents construct addicts as irresponsible children. They are liars who cannot be trusted because they are focused only on their next "fix." By labeling people addicts, we cement their flawed character. They are, first and foremost, addicts. "Addict" becomes their dominant identity, their "master status";[7] every aspect of their lives is considered a consequence of their addiction, and every aspect must be changed if their addiction is to be cured. How habitual substance users view themselves and their substance use is considered irrelevant. They are liars and can't be trusted. If they talk about the pleasures of drug use, it is their "addiction" talking, their addicted self. Our inability to stop drug use shows us that there is much we don't understand about the benefits of drug use. If it were all harm and pain, why would people continue using drugs?

Treatment Is the Only Path to Abstinence

Allied with our belief in the value of sobriety is our understanding that abstinence from drugs can be achieved only through treatment. The idea that formal treatment is the only way to stop habitual substance use is so widespread that we rarely consider evidence to the contrary. The few scholars who have studied the phenomena of "natural recovery" have found that habitual substance users who don't go to treatment fare as well as, and in some cases better than, their drug-using counterparts who attend treatment.[8] The sociologists Robert Granfield and William Cloud have coined the term "recovery capital" to describe the aspects of habitual substance users' lives that they rely on to help them stop, or control, their drug use on their own.[9] One of the first steps for this process is the substance user's rejection of the dominant paradigm of addiction, namely that it's a disease that encompasses one's entire life, the cure for which is drug treatment. Because these substance users reject this definition of addiction, they understand themselves as having control over their substance use in ways foreclosed by the disease model; their substance use is one part, not the whole, of their lives. They don't necessarily identify as "addicts"—an identity that the dominant paradigm of addiction has made all encompassing. They don't believe they're sick with a chronic, incurable disease. This belief that addiction is incurable might create the reality it attempts to explain.

The persistent faith in treatment is widespread. For years, it has been the mantra of drug policy reformers, myself included. Our hope was that it could shift emphasis away from law enforcement's role in the problem of drugs and help reorient us toward humane approaches that understood addiction as a disease best addressed with treatment, not force. We wanted drug users who want treatment to be able to access it without having to be arrested first. At the 2009 International Drug Policy Reform Conference, many participants began to question their oft-repeated mantra "treatment not incarceration" as we heard about the Obama administration's plans for expanding drug courts and coerced treatment. The assumption has been that treatment, even when coerced, is better than incarceration. The hope of drug policy reformers was, in part, that drug courts were a step toward removing control of drug users from the criminal justice system altogether, a step toward dismantling the War on Drugs. What many did not anticipate was the way this powerful institution would adopt a treatment paradigm to justify expanded, not reduced, criminal justice oversight of drug users. Drug court advocates, as I showed in chapter 3, are interested in reforming the criminal justice system, not in minimizing its involvement in the lives of drug users. Drug courts are predicated on the criminalization of drugs. Without this criminalization, they have no way to recruit clients. President Obama touts the benefits of rehabilitation while submitting a drug control budget similar to that of his predecessor; his drug czar publicly distances himself from the *language* of the War on Drugs while making imperceptible changes to its actual implementation. Treatment and punishment are not distinct strategies for dealing with drug users, but are now complements in an expanding system of social control where defendants are compelled to plead guilty to a crime, to admit criminality, to access treatment for a disease in a contradictory process supported by the War on Drugs framework.

Coerced Treatment Is Better

Drug court advocates argue not only that treatment is better than incarceration but that coerced treatment is better than voluntary treatment for certain addicts. They build on the widespread faith in treatment and argue that if voluntary treatment is good, then coerced treatment can only enhance its effectiveness. Drug court advocates are not arguing for the decriminalization of drugs and do not see drug courts as a way to dismantle the criminal justice system's control of drug users. Rather, they are arguing the opposite. It is because of the criminalization of drugs that addicts can get the treatment they need. They need to stay in treatment long enough for it to be effective, which they will do if coerced. And they need "swift and certain consequences" to repeated drug use while in treatment. Criminal justice reformers have adopted the belief that addiction is a disease best addressed through treatment, through a combination of carrots and sticks, and have added to this idea by arguing for the importance of coercion.

Any true reform is going to have to start with these assumptions and provide alternative conceptions of habitual substance use and substance users, sobriety and treatment, and the state's role in "curing" the drug problem. This reform must start with the acknowledgement that the problem for many drug users is their criminal justice involvement in the first place. Rather than viewing arrest as an "opportunity" to get someone into drug treatment, we must minimize the role the criminal justice system plays in drug users' lives. The first, and obvious, step is the legalization of drugs, a move supported by a wide range of advocacy organizations, criminal justice associations, and scholars. The increasing criminalization of drugs has done nothing to stop drug use and there is evidence that it does far more harm than good. Drug courts are not a step in the direction of legalization. They do nothing to decrease criminal justice oversight of drug users. Instead, they retain the criminal justice system's control of drug users and reinforce the ideology that medicine, backed by force, is the solution to addiction.

And yet legalization alone won't address the problems associated with a punitive mind-set toward drug users. Some defendants in drug court are there for drug-related offenses, and drug possession is not necessarily one of the offenses for which they've been charged. Drug policy, then, must attend to the vulnerability that surrounds some drug users' lives that stems, in part, from the fragile and eroding social service system that exists in the United States. This vulnerability might be exacerbated by drug use but it also might be mitigated by drug use. A humane approach to habitual substance use could address the vulnerability without punishing it or pretending it is the result of individual, not systemic, factors.

When drug court advocates claim that the increase in drug use and addiction has led to the mass incarceration of drug users, they ignore the nature of the criminal justice system. All illicit drug users are not equally policed, arrested, charged, convicted, and imprisoned. We know that geographic and racial disparities play an important role in the implementation of the War on Drugs; African Americans and Latinos are more likely than their white drug-using counterparts to be policed, arrested, and imprisoned for drug possession or distribution.¹⁰ Addiction has little to do with these disparities; racial bias in the criminal justice system does. Generations of families interact with the criminal justice system not because they are society's illegal drug users and addicts, but because they are monitored and policed the most. But the justification for drug courts and other therapeutic sanctions removes bias from the explanations for mass incarceration. According to this logic, addiction renders people vulnerable to criminal justice involvement, not racism. By misdiagnosing the problem, they prescribe the wrong medicine.

While many organizations argue for the legalization of drugs, they are simultaneously trying to offer an alternative paradigm. Many reformers are touting a "public health" approach, tied to the medicalized one, as the solution to the drug problem. A public health perspective, they argue, acknowledges that addicts need treatment and helps to reduce the harms associated with drug use. Part of the public health approach then, which frames addiction not as an individual illness but a societal problem, involves the creation of the "epidemic" or crisis of addiction as a call to action. It is a matter of public health if it is viewed as a threat at the level of the population. The National Institute on Drug Abuse has adopted this public health argument, explaining that "addiction affects everyone. . . . Directly or indirectly every community is affected by drug abuse and addiction, as is every family member."¹¹ To emphasize this point, they link addiction to cancer, heart disease, HIV/AIDS, violence, stress, and child abuse. They claim that addiction costs the United States $484 billion per year. The National Institute of Medicine has repeated this public health mantra. The new head of the Substance Abuse and Mental Health Services Administration argues that addiction is not just an individual illness but affects "entire populations."¹² The move is to emphasize that addiction is a crisis for which an expanded treatment system is the best solution. But, as NIDA reminds us, the public health approach is not antithetical to a criminalized one: "Treatment in a criminal justice setting can succeed in preventing an offender's return to criminal behavior, particularly when treatment continues as the person transitions back into the community."¹³

The public health model still embodies many of the assumptions that underpin drug courts. Addiction, as a disease, greatly affects society; it is a public health problem whose solution is expanded treatment. If this treatment must be forced, this is still justified within a public health model because the societal costs of addiction justify this coercion. The public health model contains potential to move us away from the criminal justice model. But it could be used to justify the criminal justice system on the assumption that people need treatment, even and especially those who deny they have a problem in the first place. Public health rationales, often justified in terms of "risky" behaviors, contain within them the belief that people *can* and *should* control themselves to adhere to norms. Disease is something that can be avoided, in part, through self-control and "reasonable" behavior. Health, then, becomes not merely the absence of disease but rather a state to be pursued; the healthful person is moral, controlled, and self-governing.[14] Public health rationales contain within them the logic of personal responsibility that can lend themselves to a punitive orientation if, for example, addicts don't actively pursue treatment, and by extension, sobriety.[15]

If treatment is available and works, addicts are obliged to seek it out. It is their duty, and if they don't seek it out on their own, then the state has an obligation to, literally, force health on them. Public health logics constitute their own form of social power, where personal responsibility and state control are fused in the name of moral regulation.[16] The perspective that addiction is a public health problem doesn't inherently remove it from criminal justice oversight, especially if it is fused with precisely the principles of personal responsibility and control that form the basis for drug and other "problem-solving" courts.

The public health approach is fueling the medical marijuana movement, which has had some success toward the decriminalization of this particular drug. To date, fourteen states have legalized medical marijuana as a treatment for arthritis, cancer, and glaucoma, and as a powerful pain medication. In many other states, possession is considered a misdemeanor and punishable by only a fine. For the first time in its history, the American Medical Association has acknowledged that marijuana has medicinal use; it is also supported by the American College of Physicians and other prominent medical organizations. Advocates of medical marijuana have made considerable efforts to reframe this drug as an effective medicine. The medical establishment, then, is in control of its justification and dispensation. This approach is a form of decriminalization, allowing people who *need* the drug for *medically legitimate* reasons to access it. This loosening of the laws around marijuana could be seen as a first step toward liberalizing our approach to drugs more generally in the United States, heralding a new approach. Proposition 19, the Regulate, Control, and Tax Cannabis

Act recently on the ballot in California, was an attempt to move away from the medical marijuana framework by proposing the legalization of small quantities of marijuana and the regulation of its distribution. While the proposition was defeated in November 2, 2010, 47% of the voters were in favor of marijuana's legalization, suggesting that there is strong support for transforming the laws around cannabis use and distribution.

The application of these loosening marijuana laws suggests, however, that this liberalization is only partial and potentially fraught with the same racial bias that characterizes the criminal justice system as a whole. Harry Levine and Deborah Small recently documented the dramatic increase in marijuana-related arrests in New York City despite the decriminalization of marijuana possession.[17] They found that in 2007, the NYPD arrested almost 40,000 people, up from 3,200 in 1987, for the crime of having marijuana open to public view. Of those arrested, the majority were African American and Latino men. Levine and Small argue that these arrests, in the face of a general decline in the criminalization of marijuana, serve as an institutionalized form of surveillance for poor young men of color, allowing the police to collect their fingerprints and enter them into the city's criminal justice database. These arrests are also easy for police who target poorer neighborhoods to make; once arrested, people are compelled to plead guilty, leading to criminal justice sanctions for marijuana possession.

The movement toward medical marijuana also has the potential to perpetuate the distinctions we make between good and bad drug use and users. Good drug use is that which has been deemed medically necessary; bad drug use is that which is done despite the harms associated with it. Good drug users get their medicine from doctors while bad ones obtain it illegally. When I ask my students their views on drug policy, they almost uniformly support marijuana's legalization; they rarely support the legalization of other "hard" drugs, however, arguing that their effects make them too dangerous. Marijuana users, whom they are or know, should not be punished for their drug use, but heroin or crack users, whom they claim not to know, should be. Medical marijuana's expansion does not necessarily represent the paradigmatic shift that could move us away from needing to designate certain drug users as bad, and from then acting with force on these bad drug users. Medical marijuana is predicated on a medical justification for its value. Drug courts use a medical logic, addiction as disease, to justify their value.

The public health and medical models, while attempts to move away from the criminalized perspective on drug use, still retain the emphasis on drug use as a *problem* that needs to be *fixed* through *treatment*. The perspective that holds the most hope for moving away from these assumptions, which have been so readily adopted by the criminal justice system at the same time that they're being used as a justification for its dismantling, is the harm reduction perspective. Harm reduction is based on the idea that drug use is and will remain a part of society, regardless of whether we agree with it morally, philosophically, medically, or legally. Harm reduction, as its name implies, accepts that people use drugs and attempts to minimize the harms associated with these drugs, including the harms caused by the criminal justice system. One of harm reduction's central tenets is that drug users should be treated in a nonjudgmental and noncoercive way; they should not be forced into any form of treatment, and the goal of any services provided to drug users should be to help them reduce the harms that can be associated with their drug use, without requiring abstinence from drugs to receive these services or punishing them if they continue to use drugs. Also, rather than assuming drug users negatively influence one another, harm reduction accepts that they can also teach one another to minimize the harms that can be associated with drug use.

Through a nonjudgmental acceptance of drug use, harm reduction provides a very different framework for understanding habitual substance use. Because sobriety is not its main goal, treatment is not heralded as the only solution to drug use and coercion is explicitly avoided. Examples of this approach include drug consumption rooms, several of which exist in Switzerland, Germany, Norway, Denmark, and the Netherlands, where people can use illegal drugs without fear of arrest.[18] Safe injecting facilities, in Australia and Vancouver, provide clean needles and a medically supervised site for injection drug users.[19] The goal of these projects is to reduce health-related harms, such as overdose and the negative consequences of using dirty needles, but also to reduce the negative consequences of public drug consumption, including arrest. In Vancouver, the safe injecting site, still in its "pilot project" phase, has become a resource for police, some of whom refer people to the site.[20] Clearly, these spaces are predicated on a very different approach to drug use, seeing the harm associated with drugs in a very different light than the harm presented by drug court and criminal justice proponents, who view arrest as the "opportunity" to treat an addict, as the chance to change them into the sober productive citizens the criminal justice system wants them to be.[21]

Harm reduction as a philosophy has grown out of a practice focused on addressing the specific needs of drug users in the face of structural barriers, including their criminalization. Heroin injecting rooms and the provision of clean needles are practices that accept drug use and facilitate its safe consumption—safe understood not just in relation to concepts of health but in terms of the harms associated with policing and arrest. Harm reduction is predicated on the idea that drug users know what's best for themselves; sound practice and policy must take into account their perspectives if it is to effectively address their needs. As Alan Clear, the executive director of the Harm Reduction Coalition recently explained to me, "Harm reduction is both a philosophy and a specific approach. It is, first, a way of involving people who use drugs in the dialogue." It draws on the "collective wisdom of people who use drugs," and in doing so counters the dominant understanding of drug users echoed by drug court advocates, configured as "addicts," as irrational and thus delegitimized as possible experts on drug use. The New York Users Union, formed in 2005, echoes the idea that drug users need to be part of the drug policy conversation and seeks to affect drug policy, in part by drawing on its members' identification as current or former drug users.[22] These and other groups, based on the harm reduction perspective, seek to affect policy by both lessening the deleterious effects of criminalization while also advocating for the legalization of drugs.

A harm reduction perspective also transforms traditional ways of thinking about treatment. Treatment isn't the only path to abstinence from drugs, and abstinence does not need to be the ultimate goal of drug treatment. Howard Josepher, a longtime drug treatment expert, argues that we should move away from the language of "clean and sober" to that of "health and well-being" when talking about drug users.[23] Further, he argues, "the whole world of addiction is a very black-and-white, clean-and-dirty world. . . . A more inclusive definition of recovery means that we start to take the world of addiction out of black and white and define a gray area, where most of life exists."[24] The goal then of non-abstinence-focused drug treatment programs is to help people, who have arrived there voluntarily, to define what success would mean in terms of achievable outcomes, often defined as managed drug use, instead of outcomes, such as abstinence, that are difficult for many and impossible for some to achieve.

As we rethink drug policy, we must ultimately dismantle our preoccupation with drugs and sobriety, cleanliness and dirt, and the false di-
chotomies we maintain and reify between the natural drug-free versus the
contaminated drug-using body.[25] The label "drug user" ushers in a host of
disciplinary practices over the bodies of people designated as such. Harm
reduction, with its questioning of these practices, has the potential to reframe our point of reference. Ultimately, though, these practices must be
accompanied by a cultural shift away from an ideology that valorizes sobriety as the ultimate measure of one's worth and the ultimate sign that
one's willpower has been effectively exercised for the sake of one's self and
others, and that moves away from calling people who use drugs "drug users," as if this is the whole of their identity. Perhaps we should not ask what
should be done about the "drug problem," but rather what should be done
about our obsession with drugs as a problem, and the problems this has
caused for those coerced into sobriety "for their own good."

Force Is Not the Best Medicine

The recent critiques of drug courts eerily resemble those that led to the demise of Progressive Era courts. Drug courts are procedurally inconsistent;
not everyone is able to access them, either because they are not available
in all jurisdictions or because eligibility criteria differ across jurisdictions.[26]
People convicted of violent crimes are excluded from most drug courts,
and many don't accept people with a diagnosed mental illness. One effect of these inconsistent eligibility criteria is a process called "skimming,"
where drug courts are avoiding people labeled "high-risk," leading to differential treatment within the system. It was this same differential treatment, and the individual discretion it entailed, that dismantled Progressive
Era reforms.

Second, and related to this skimming effect, is the charge that drug
courts are racially biased. While African Americans have been dispropor-
tionately affected by the War on Drugs, they are often screened out of eligibility for drug courts because of prior convictions, which they are more
likely to have because of racial bias.[27] Poor defendants often have a hard
time completing drug treatment, lacking the resources necessary to fulfill the drug court program's requirements while dealing with the effects
of poverty. These defendants, then, often end up spending more time in

prison than if they had bypassed drug court: they spend time in the drug court and treatment and then in prison, having failed at the treatment and having a certain prison sentence awaiting them because they had to plead guilty to access the drug court in the first place.

A third, and related, critique lobbied against drug courts is that they are "conviction mills," requiring people to plead guilty to access them, often with little time to consider the consequences of this decision.[28] This truncation of the "discovery process," when the defendant's attorney reviews the case and the options for his or her client, means that defense counsel often is not able to give the defendant any advice before they enter this guilty plea. In many instances, drug court participants are not represented by a defense attorney in any substantive way. In some jurisdictions, if defendants choose to enter into this discovery period, they are automatically excluded from drug court. This means, for example, that if they want to fight the basis for their arrest and begin to do so, drug courts are no longer an option for them. Once they've entered this guilty plea, they will have a prison sentence for a felony drug conviction if they fail at drug court, and yet this plea is the only way to get into most drug courts. Critiques against Progressive Era courts were very similar; the merger of this helping and punishing function meant that the adversarial quality of the court, where defendants could be protected, was eroded, often to the defendants' detriment. This was the price they paid for "help."

And the fourth critique emerging about drug courts, perhaps the most devastating to their claims to be an "alternative" to incarceration, is that they "widen the net" of those under criminal justice supervision, increasing the number of people monitored by the punishment system.[29] Drug courts often process "discretionary crimes" that police might not have enforced had drug court not been an option. Prosecutors might pursue a case because they have drug court as an option where they would have dismissed it without this alternative. Progressive Era courts were critiqued for this same effect; they widened the scope of offenses deemed punishable, developed specialized courts for treating them, and institutionalized adults and children who would not have been under criminal justice supervision had there not been a place to put them and way to categorize them within this punitive system.

Rather than constituting a new moment in punishment, drug courts hark back to the time, most evident in the Progressive Era, when personal transformation via coercion was considered the enlightened way to deal with the problems of crime and punishment. As in the Progressive Era, drug court advocates are, for the most part, convinced that the system that punishes can also heal. They believe that the medical and punitive logics are not contradictory, and when combined, can be especially effective at "transforming lives" and "saving souls." Further, they believe that by relying on what the "science" tells us about addiction, they are ensuring that their efforts are immune to the perversions that have plagued past attempts at reform.

The historian David Rothman has written that Progressive Era reformers:

> were convinced their innovation could satisfy *all* goals, that the same person and the same institution could at once guard and help, protect and rehabilitate, maintain custody and deliver treatment. They perceived no conflict between these goals, no clash of interest between the deviant and wider society, between the warden and his convicts, between the hospital superintendent and his patients, between the keeper and the kept. . . . This belief was among the most fundamental in the reformers' canon, and in retrospect perhaps the most dubious. The study of the past does not give license to predict the future, but it is more than a little tempting to argue that such goals can never be satisfied together, that they are too diametrically opposed, at least in this society, to be joined.[30]

Coerced therapeutic sanctions, as they have reemerged and expanded to increasing aspects of human life, offer an opportunity to consider the multifaceted and complex way that punishment, surveillance, and control are enacted through a variety of seemingly contradictory mechanisms. Medicalization, often touted as a humane approach to deviance, actually strengthens the criminal justice system's hold over social problems. The criminal justice system contributes to this medicalization process, creating theories about addiction, coercion, and recovery that are, in fact, specific to the criminal justice system's preoccupation with certain types of behavior change for specific individuals.

Considering drug courts as something different and apart from the prison ironically allowed me to understand them as complementary, rather than opposed, to prison's concentrated, enclosed system. The historical studies of punishment make clear that unless and until we decouple the general logic of punishment and specific criminal justice strategies—however benign-seeming or well-motivated or scientifically informed they may be—from social phenomena such as drug use, we will endlessly repeat the cycle of conscience and convenience that has been, to date, punishment's hallmark. Given the strong and dominant faith in the disease model of addiction, the effectiveness of treatment, the importance of sobriety, and the value of coercion, it seems likely that drug courts will withstand these critiques. But it is equally likely that they will do nothing to stop the expansion of the criminal justice system or the punitive way we understand drug users, despite our faith in the medical model and therapeutic paradigms. And they will do little to stop illicit drug use. Force *is* the best medicine because we are ideologically committed to the idea that punishment and treatment work, despite historical and contemporary evidence to the contrary.

Appendix

GROUNDED IN THE sociology of knowledge,[1] I have sought to answer the following questions: (1) How are the seemingly contradictory approaches to drug use—therapeutic and punitive—merged in the concept of drug courts? (2) What knowledge do drug court advocates draw on to reconstruct the problem of addiction and articulate a role for the courts in solving social problems? (3) What theories about addiction, treatment, and the problem-solving role of the criminal justice system do drug court advocates construct to justify and expand their institution's scope?

To accomplish this broader approach to studying drug courts, I designed a project that allowed me to look at the knowledge construction around the drug court field. My central research strategies have consisted of: (1) the analysis of documents generated by the advocacy organizations, governmental agencies, and research centers concerned with drug courts and their expansion; and (2) interviews with key members of these organizations. I have also attended one annual drug court conference and two American Society of Criminology conferences, where I attended entire panels devoted to presenting the results of drug court evaluation research. I conducted content analysis of these various data sources to see how the problem of addiction was constructed, and how a clear role for the courts and coercion was articulated in these constructions.

Document Analysis

Much of my analysis has centered on documents published by the two main drug court advocacy organizations: the National Association of Drug Court Professionals (NADCP) and its offshoot, the National Drug Court Institute (NDCI). NADCP formed in 1994 to "represent drug court professionals on Capitol Hill," and created NDCI, in 1997, through funds from the White House's Office of National Drug Control Policy, to focus on drug court research and technical assistance and training. Combined, these two organizations publish several types of documents, including a quarterly professional newsletter, practitioner fact sheets, the *National Drug Court Institute Review* journal, a monograph series covering a variety of drug court issues, and an annual overview of drug court research. At the request of the federal government, both organizations are involved in drafting the Model Drug Offender Accountability and Treatment Act, which would require states to incorporate drug court practices throughout the criminal justice system and all drug offenders to undergo a screening for addiction.[2] All documents published by NADCP and NDCI are available through their respective websites. Several governmental organizations concerned with criminal justice issues write about and promote drug courts, often drawing their information from NADCP or NDCI publications, many of which they have funded. Combined, I analyzed these documents for how they construct the problem of substance use and the role of courts in solving this problem.

The second major organization that has put considerable effort into promoting drug courts is the Center for Court Innovation. Located in New York City, the staff of this organization helped to start one of the first drug courts, the Brooklyn Treatment Court, and has spent considerable time writing about the "problem-solving court revolution" generally. The documents published by this organization include books, journal articles, and "think pieces," many commissioned by NADCP. Because this organization is actively involved in promoting drug courts, they make their documents readily available through their websites, and I have accessed these documents when possible.

Drug courts have moved from a small practice to a national one—all part of what advocates call their "institutionalization." For this reason, in recent years they have published many documents outlining drug court institutionalization, where they articulate (and sometimes debate) what institutionalization should look like. As Peter Berger and Thomas Luckmann write, "Theoretically sophisticated legitimations appear at particular moments of an institutional history."[3] Accordingly, many of the documents I analyzed represented concerted efforts by advocates to describe and advance the drug court field, at a particular time when discussions of their expansion and incorporation into "mainstream criminal justice practice" have figured prominently. This has been a particularly good time to study drug courts, as they expand their activities and as drug court advocates engage in reflections on this expansion. NADCP and the Center for Court Innovation have commissioned several works on the future of drug courts and their institutionalization, a theme echoed in several of the presentations at their annual conference, which I attended in 2004. This shift from

"noble experiment" to "an enduring part of the criminal justice system's response to the problems of drug addiction and crime" is the source of much
reflection by drug court advocates that has served as a crucial source of
data for this book.[4]

A central tool advocates use to argue for drug court expansion is research on the efficacy of coerced treatment. Andrew Abbott argues that
research can play a key role in staking professional territory by legitimating activities and providing a "central foundation for jurisdiction," without
which institutions are vulnerable to attack.[5] Importantly, as Robert Alford
argues, the "abstract and seemingly neutral tone" of institutional reports
masks their underlying ideological purpose.[6] The evaluation research represents a clear attempt to operationalize many of the drug court's goals—
"behavior change"[7] and "creat[ing] productive citizens"[8]—into measurable
elements such as recidivism rates. The conclusions of these evaluations,
however, often extend beyond the measures used in the study, to make
broader arguments about drug courts and coerced treatment. While these
evaluations have been used frequently to argue for the expansion of drug
courts and the benefits of treatment over prison, they are increasingly being used by advocates to argue for the benefits of coercion over voluntary
participation in treatment.[9] These studies are also being used to argue for
the importance of an enhanced judicial role in addressing substance use
and against drug policy reforms that seek to minimize the criminal justice
system's control over illicit drug users.[10] I analyzed the most prominent of
these drug court evaluation studies to examine how conclusions about the
effects of drug courts are derived, and to investigate the ideological perspectives on drug use and addiction underlying the neutral language of
empirical research. Because there are an enormous number of drug court
evaluations published regularly, I focused my analysis on the research conducted and published by the major national research organizations.

Interviews

The second research strategy I employed was interviews with key drug court
advocates. For this phase of the research I used a "purposeful sampling" pro-
cedure, a "strategy in which particular settings, persons or events are selected
deliberately in order to provide important information that can't be gotten as
well from other choices."[11] I was not interested in a random sample of people

involved in the drug court field, but rather those who have played an important role in advancing drug courts at the national level.

I identified "key" advocates in two main ways: first, I looked at the organizations devoted to drug court expansion and identified people in those organizations who have been actively involved in writing about and promoting drug courts. For the second approach, I employed a "snowball sampling" technique, whereby I asked each person I interviewed to recommend other people to interview whom they identified as important figures in the drug court field.[12] As H. Russell Bernard points out, this sampling technique is especially effective "when you are dealing with a relatively small population of people who are likely to be in contact with one another."[13] This is an apt description of the drug court field, where there are many people working on the local level on drug courts but a relatively small number of people involved, at the national level, in articulating the knowledge used to bolster drug courts.

Overall, I conducted twelve interviews with people I identified as key figures in the knowledge construction of drug courts. Described in the methods literature as "elite interviewing," I purposely chose "well-informed people . . . on the basis of their expertise in areas relevant to the research."[14] This type of interviewing has distinct advantages with a research project such as mine, focused on the knowledge construction of an institutional field. The disadvantage, however, is that the elites are often reluctant to speak beyond the "party line" when being interviewed, especially when they know that their name is going to be attached to the interview data.

While I was distinctly interested in the "party line," I was also hoping to hear advocates say things that they might not be willing or eager to in official advocacy reports, papers, books, and articles. For this reason, I chose to offer the interviewees anonymity. The advantage to promising anonymity is that it allowed me to hear critiques (occasionally quite strong ones) of drug courts and coerced treatment that simply would not be permissible in drug court advocacy documents. During several interviews, which I audiotaped, interviewees would start to say something, ask me again if their names were going to be used, and when I said no would proceed to tell me something they did not feel comfortable saying "on the record." For this reason, I firmly believe the choice to offer anonymity was a wise one, because it allowed me to gain important insights into some of the pragmatic and, sometimes, philosophical issues advocates were grappling with, and their ambiguity about certain aspects of coerced drug treatment. When I do attach an advocate's name to something stated or written about drug courts, this is when I am quoting from a document that is publicly available and to which the advocate's name is associated as author.

There is, however, a major disadvantage to offering advocates anonymity. This mainly has to do with a "flattening effect"[15] that this approach produces. Throughout this book, I refer to my interviewees as "drug court advocates" or "proponents," yet the reader will not be able to know more about any particular person and, importantly, her or his position in the drug court field. And given the relative dearth of organizations promoting drug courts nationally, I must be careful with identifying comments that can clue the reader into what kind of organization the person interviewing works for and her or his relationship to the day-to-day operations of any particular drug court. The way I have attempted to deal with this problem is by interviewing people who are active in the drug court field. Thus all the people I interviewed have written or spoken extensively about drug courts. What I have gained is a perspective not available in the normal venues in which these people talk about drug courts, but what is lost is the specificity of who exactly is speaking. This does pose a barrier when one is writing about knowledge at the institutional level, but I remain convinced that anonymity allowed me to see some ambiguities and ambivalence I would not have had access to otherwise.

I designed a semi-structured interview format but left the line of questioning fairly open. The purpose of the interviews was to understand the interviewee's involvement with drug courts, the problem they believed that drug courts were responding to, their understanding of addiction and how they learned about it and drug treatment, their experience garnering support for drug courts both inside and outside the criminal justice system, their perspectives on other possible policy approaches to dealing with the "problem of drugs," and lastly, their perspectives on the "institutionalization" of the drug court field and what "success" would look like. Inevitably, we would talk about other things, often drug court practice and where one "draws the line" in terms of the judge's incursion into a defendant's life.

Data Analysis

To analyze the data, I have used a "grounded theory" approach, where my theoretical perspectives on drug courts have been developed "in constant interaction with the data from the study."[16] To clarify, because it is my experience that grounded theory can be a misunderstood approach, this does not mean I began the formal stage of this research without theoretical perspectives on coerced drug treatment. As I developed, initiated, and completed this project (and I consider writing my findings as part of this ongoing work), I continually move back and forth from the empirical and theoretical tracks of analysis. Robert Alford has explained that "the way out of either empiricism or theoreticism is to see the two tracks of analysis as dialectically interrelated throughout the process of inquiry."[17] However, as Alford further explains, "the theoretical and empirical aspects of a problem are thus always in tension with each other. Abstract concepts never perfectly fit the complexity of reality."[18] I move between documenting the written and spoken words of the drug court advocates, but I use them not as windows onto the "truth" of drug courts but, rather, as perspectives that can help in understanding the historical, social, and theoretical significance of the reemergence of rehabilitative sanctions.

Ultimately, I have "combine[d] an empirical focus on the language and gesture of human interactions with a theoretical concern with their symbolic meaning."[19] By focusing on the "ideologies, discourses, and cultural frameworks" of the drug court advocates, I have analyzed their words in an attempt to understand the "symbolic meaning" and "cultural significance" of the reemergence of rehabilitative sanctions. To do so, I also consider part of my "data" the historical work on punishment and the medicalization of social problems. I have used this historical work analytically and theoretically—analytically, to help understand the reemergence of therapeutic sanctions; theoretically, to help me construct broader arguments about where drug courts fit in with the large-scale history of punishment.

Notes

Notes to the Introduction

1. Kolbert, "A Drug Court Takes a Risk to Aid Addicts."
2. Finkelstein, "New York to Offer Most Addicts Treatment Instead of Jail Terms."
3. See, for example, Lay, "Rehab Justice"; Satel, "For Addicts, Firm Hand Can Be the Best Medicine."
4. Satel, "For Addicts, Firm Hand Can Be the Best Medicine."
5. Maron, "Courting Drug-Policy Reform."
6. See, for example, King and Pasquarella, "Drug Courts"; Orr et al., "America's Problem-Solving Courts." These reports are far more critical than most reports on drug courts, and expose important problems with drug courts. Despite what are often quite extensive (and damning) critiques, both reports end with suggestions for improving drug court procedures to remove the problems the authors identify.
7. Burns and Peyrot, "Tough Love"; Nolan, *Reinventing Justice.*
8. Tiger and Finkelstein, "The Public Policy Context of Drug Use in New York City," 256.
9. SAMHSA, "Characteristics of Young Adult (Aged 18–25) and Youth (Aged 12–17) Admissions"; SAMHSA, "Treatment Episodes Data Set (TEDS) Highlights."
10. NADCP, "From the Chief Executive's Desk."
11. Feeley and Simon, "New Penology"; Garland, *Culture of Control.* While many authors have noted this trend, Feeley, Simon, and Garland are often credited with establishing this as a dominant perspective within the sociology of punishment. Garland, in his important book *Punishment and Modern Social Theory*, helped to establish the sociology of punishment as a distinct field from disciplines such as criminology; his goal was, in part, to articulate punishment as a *social* practice with important historical origins and cultural ramifications.
12. Erikson, *Wayward Puritans*; Gorski, *Disciplinary Revolution.*
13. Rothman's *Conscience and Convenience* was the first book to examine the history of prison and Progressive Era responses to it in the United States.
14. The sociologist James Nolan, in both *Reinventing Justice* and "Drug Treatment Courts and the Disease Paradigm," writes about drug courts as if they are revolutionary rather than a repeat of Progressive Era reforms. One of his arguments against making this comparison (which I employ here) is that

the disease paradigm advanced by drug courts is distinct from the ideas that motivated Progressive Era court reformers. While Nolan's data and analyses are quite strong, I think he overstates his case of drug courts' uniqueness and understates their important historical continuity with earlier punishment forms, specifically, and broader ideas about deviance, more generally.

15. Gorski's *Disciplinary Revolution* is a concise and persuasive argument for understanding the role that discipline has played in the formation of the modern state. Gorski argues that discipline was a mode of moral regulation and social control essential to creating the order necessary for state building. Surveillance and discipline are two important features of what he refers to as the "disciplinary revolution" that underpinned modern state formation. As a historical sociologist, Gorski turns a necessary lens to historical processes that are the precursors to modern disciplinary regimes, while also arguing that the way discipline manifests itself at any one historical moment is not merely a repeat of the past.

16. King and Pasquarella, "Drug Courts"; Drug Policy Alliance, "Drug Courts Are Not the Answer"; O'Hear, "Rethinking Drug Courts"; Orr et al., "America's Problem-Solving Courts." The critiques that are emerging about drug courts suggest that drug courts are moving toward the phase of critique that prison and Progressive Era courts did in earlier eras. The emergence of these critiques provides further strength to Rothman's arguments in *Conscience and Convenience*: punishment forms move in cycles where they are considered reforms motivated by conscience to administrative routines that fail to meet their promises of humanizing punishment.

Notes to Chapter 1

1. Burns and Peyrot, "Tough Love."
2. As quoted in Nolan, *Reinventing Justice*, 71.
3. HBO, "Addiction," http://www.hbo.com/addiction/; Jensen, "Facing 'Things That Destroy Your Life.'"
4. Jensen, Facing 'Things That Destroy Your Life.'"
5. Burns and Peyrot, "Tough Love."
6. As quoted in ibid., 422.
7. Olson et al., "Implementing the Key Components of Specialized Treatment Courts"; Spohn et al., "Drug Courts and Recidivism."
8. Drug Courts Program Office, "About the Drug Courts Program Office."
9. Snavely, "Critical Need for Jail as a Sanction in the Drug Court Model."
10. Burns and Peyrot, "Tough Love"; Fox and Huddleston, "Drug Courts in the U.S."; Kassebaum and Okamoto, "Drug Court a Sentencing Model"; Nolan, *Reinventing Justice*; Nolan, "Therapeutic Adjudication."
11. Huddleston and Marlowe, "Painting the Current Picture."

12. NADCP, "Facts on Drug Courts," http://www.nadcp.org/whatis/.
13. Ibid.
14. GAO, "Adult Drug Courts."
15. Ibid., 37.
16. Huddleston and Marlowe, "Painting the Current Picture."
17. Drug Courts Program Office, "About the Drug Courts Program Office."
18. Fox and Wolf, "Future of Drug Courts."
19. Butts, "Introduction."
20. Johnson, "Choice of Drug Czar Indicates Focus on Treatment Not Jail."
21. COPS, "One-on-One with ONDCP Director Gil Kerlikowske."
22. Piper, "Obama's Drug War Budget Looks a Lot Like Bush's."
23. NADCP, "All Rise."
24. Gillie and Huddleston, "All Rise!"
25. Eckholm, "Innovative Courts Give Some Addicts the Chance to Straighten Out."
26. von Zielbauer, "Court Treatment System Is Found to Help Drug Offenders Stay Clean."
27. Eckholm, "Innovative Courts Give Some Addicts the Chance to Straighten Out"; von Zielbauer, "Court Treatment System Is Found to Help Drug Offenders Stay Clean"; Wren, "New Court Lets Drug Addicts Choose Treatment Program Rather Than Jail."
28. Wren, "New Court Lets Drug Addicts Choose Treatment Program Rather Than Jail."
29. Rempel et al., "Drug Courts an Effective Treatment Alternative."
30. Ibid.
31. Ibid.
32. Cissner and Rempel, "State of Drug Court Research," 1.
33. Ibid.
34. Ibid., 4–5.
35. Ibid., 7.
36. Ibid, 7–9.
37. Drug Policy Alliance, "Drug Courts Are Not the Answer," 12.
38. BJS, "Correctional Population in the United States, Annual Prisoners in 2008."
39. BJS, "Probation and Parole in the United States, 2007."
40. Conrad and Schneider, *Deviance and Medicalization*; May, "Pathology, Identity, and the Social Construction of Alcohol Dependence."
41. Musto, *American Disease.*
42. Nolan, *Reinventing Justice.*
43. Garland, *Culture of Control*; Mauer, "Causes and Consequences of Prison Growth in the United States."

44. Acker, *Creating the American Junkie*, 2.
45. Musto, *American Disease*, 278.
46. Tunnell's *Pissing on Demand* extensively documents this expansion in workplace drug testing in both the federal government and private industry. Tunnell shows how the surveillance of drug testing is an oft-overlooked part of the War on Drugs and one that that will affect many (if not most) people in the United States at one point in their lives.
47. Acker, *Creating the American Junkie*.
48. Mauer, "Causes and Consequences of Prison Growth in the United States."
49. Tonry, *Malign Neglect*.
50. Garriott, *Policing Methamphetamine*, 34.
51. Global Commission on Drugs, "War on Drugs."
52. Please see the appendix for a full description of my study's methods.
53. Berger and Luckmann, *Social Construction of Reality*.
54. See, for example, Belenko, "Research on Drug Courts"; Goldkamp et al., "Do Drug Courts Work?"; Spohn et al., "Drug Courts and Recidivism."
55. See, for example, Goldkamp et al., "Do Drug Courts Work?"
56. Burns and Peyrot, "Tough Love"; Nolan, *Reinventing Justice*; Paik, *Discretionary Justice*.
57. Satel, "For Addicts, Firm Hand Can Be the Best Medicine."
58. Christie, "Changes in Penal Values"; Rothman, *Conscience and Convenience*.
59. Martinson, "What Works?"
60. Alford, *Craft of Inquiry*.
61. Swidler and Arditi, "New Sociology of Knowledge."
62. Abbott, *System of Professions*.
63. Best, *Threatened Children*; Gusfield, *Contested Meanings*.
64. Gusfield, "Journey with Symbolic Interaction."
65. Gusfield, *Culture of Public Problems*, 18.
66. Best, *Threatened Children*.
67. Garland, *Culture of Control*; Hook, "Discourse, Knowledge, Materiality, History"; Rose, *Governing the Soul*.
68. Hook, "Discourse, Knowledge, Materiality, History."
69. Foucault, *Discipline and Punish*.
70. Garland, *Punishment and Modern Society*; Simon, *Poor Discipline*.
71. Alford, *Craft of Inquiry*.
72. Friedland and Alford, in "Bringing Society Back In," introduce the idea of "contradictory institutional logics" to describe situations where institutions with different governing logics converge in their jurisdiction over particular issues. In some respects, drug courts are the ideal embodiment of these contradictory institutional logics, with punishment and treatment representing polar opposite perspectives on how to "fix" deviance. However, in practice,

both have been intertwined from their inception despite conceptual and institutional differences. And both perspectives agree that habitual substance use is a problem that must be fixed. Friedland and Alford also suggest that when two institutions with contradictory logics merge, the one with the socially dominant logic might prevail; the meeting is rarely between equals.

73. Platt's *Child Savers* and Willrich's *City of Courts* are two examples of scholarly work that is attentive to narratives of progress when writing about Progressive Era reforms. They explicitly avoid judgment as to the merits of these reforms, but instead advise caution when assuming that reforms labeled "progressive" are inherently better ways of managing deviance.

74. Gusfield, *Culture of Public Problems*, 192. Gusfield was instrumental in articulating the idea that the study of social problems should be approached critically and for the purpose of positing other, possibly as yet unimagined, ways of viewing phenomena cast as social problems.

Notes to Chapter 2

1. Rothman, *Conscience and Convenience*.
2. Gorski, *Disciplinary Revolution*.
3. Ibid.
4. Rothman, *The Discovery of the Asylum*, xxii.
5. Ibid, xxvi.
6. Ibid, xxix.
7. Erikson, *Wayward Puritans*, 17.
8. Becker, *Outsiders*; Goffman, *Stigma*.
9. Rothman, *The Discovery of the Asylum*, xxxvii.
10. Ibid., 18–22.
11. Platt, *Child Savers*; Rothman, *Conscience and Convenience*
12. Willrich, *City of Courts*.
13. Ibid.
14. Bortner, *Inside a Juvenile Court*; Feld, *Bad Kids*; Kupchik, *Judging Juveniles*; Platt, *Child Savers*.
15. Bortner, *Inside a Juvenile Court*.
16. Feld, *Bad Kids*; see also Platt, *Child Savers*.
17. Bortner, *Inside a Juvenile Court*, 8.
18. Kupchik, *Judging Juveniles*.
19. Simon, *Poor Discipline*.
20. Nolan, *Reinventing Justice*.
21. In 1974 the sociologist Robert Martinson published a summary of a review he and colleagues had conducted of 231 published studies of "the effects of rehabilitative treatment on recidivism" ("What Works?" 24). He wrote that

they found "that with few and isolated exceptions, the rehabilitative efforts have been reported so far have had no appreciable effect on recidivism" (25). The idea that "nothing works" was quickly adopted by many in the criminal justice system eager to prove the failures of rehabilitation. The legal scholar Michael Tonry in *Malign Neglect* argues that the "mythology" that nothing works did enormous damage, prompting disinvestment in social services for offenders. Tonry points out that while Martinson and his colleagues did not find recidivism affected overall, they did find "hints here and there that particular programs had positive effects for particular kinds of offenders" (201). Martinson later tried to argue this point, but the idea that "nothing works" was already cemented into fact.

22. Beckett, *Making Crime Pay*.
23. Ibid., 5.
24. Ibid.
25. Feeley and Simon, "New Penology."
26. Simon, *Poor Discipline*.
27. Garland, *Culture of Control*.
28. Clarkson and Morgan, *Politics of Sentencing Reform*, 8.
29. Beckett and Western, "Governing Social Marginality"; Feeley and Simon, "New Penology"; Garland, *Punishment and Modern Society*; Garland, *Culture of Control*; Lynch, "Rehabilitation as Rhetoric."
30. Feeley and Simon, "New Penology," 449.
31. Ibid., 465.
32. Ibid., 479.
33. Sparks, "State Punishment in Advanced Capitalist Countries."
34. Garland, *Culture of Control*.
35. Ibid., 66.
36. Garland, *Punishment and Modern Society*.
37. Burns and Peyrot, "Tough Love"; Nolan, *Reinventing Justice*; Tiger, "Drug Courts and the Logic of Coerced Treatment."
38. For cost saving discussions, see Huddleston et al., "Painting the Current Picture"; for a discussion of drug courts' rehabilitative advantage, see Butts, "Introduction"; Satel, "For Addicts, Firm Hand Can Be the Best Medicine."

Notes to Chapter 3

1. Tonry, *Malign Neglect*.
2. King, "Disparity by Geography."
3. Berman and Feinblatt, *Good Courts*, 21.
4. Ibid., 25.
5. Ibid., 21.

6. Lieupo and Weinstein, "Ballot Initiatives," 51.
7. Ibid., 53.
8. As quoted in Fisler et al., "Edited Transcript," 13.
9. Ibid., 19.

Notes to Chapter 4

1. Conrad and Schneider, *Deviance and Medicalization*, 244.
2. Conrad, "Medicalization and Social Control"; Conrad and Schneider, *Deviance and Medicalization*; Zola, "Medicine as an Instrument of Social Control."
3. Clarke et al., "Biomedicalization."
4. Armstrong, *Conceiving Risk, Bearing Responsibility*.
5. Zola, "Medicine as an Instrument of Social Control," 404.
6. Rossol, "Medicalization of Deviance as an Interactive Achievement."
7. Ibid.
8. Clarke et al., "Biomedicalization."
9. Gusfield, "Alcohol in America."
10. Clarke et al., "Biomedicalization."
11. Hacking, *Taming of Chance*.
12. Armstrong, *Conceiving Risk, Bearing Responsibility*.
13. Conrad and Schneider, *Deviance and Medicalization*.
14. Conrad, "Medicalization and Social Control."
15. Nolan, "Drug Treatment Courts and the Disease Paradigm."
16. Peyton and Gossweiler, "Treatment Services in Adult Drug Courts."
17. Clarke et al., "Biomedicalization."
18. Ibid., 172.
19. NIDA, "Drugs, Brains, and Behavior," 5.
20. Ibid., 1.
21. Reinarman, "Addiction as Accomplishment."
22. Levine, "Discovery of Addiction."
23. Ibid., 2.
24. Valverde, *Disease of the Will*.
25. May, "Pathology, Identity, and the Social Construction of Alcohol Dependence."
26. Gusfield, *Symbolic Crusade*.
27. Reinarman, "Addiction as Accomplishment."
28. Clarke et al., "Biomedicalization."
29. Vrecko, "'Civilizing Technologies' and the Control of Deviance."
30. Keane and Hamill, "Variations in Addiction."
31. Vrecko, "'Civilizing Technologies' and the Control of Deviance."

32. Keane and Hamill, "Variations in Addiction," 54.
33. Vrecko, "'Civilizing Technologies' and the Control of Deviance."
34. Valverde, *Disease of the Will*, 11.
35. May, "Pathology, Identity, and the Social Construction of Alcohol Dependence," 395.
36. Valverde, *Disease of the Will*.
37. Nelkin, *Methadone Maintenance*, 66.
38. Attewell and Gerstein, "Government Policy and Local Practice."
39. Bourgois, "Disciplining Addictions."
40. Ibid.
41. In "The Rhetoric of Drugs," Jacques Derrida argues that the word "drug" is always "normative" and "prescriptive." It is normative in that it implies some kind of way one *should* be in relation to what is called a drug, and prescriptive in that to utter the word "drug" implies that something should be done about it and the drug user. The rhetoric of drugs (drugs not viewed as in any way a "natural" phenomena—Derrida contends that there are no drugs "in nature") takes place within an "ethico-political" framework, which implies a moral and normative stance about drugs and a political course of action (often repression but sometimes liberalization) to enact this normative perspective. The "pharmakon" refers to the duality that the word *drug* implies: natural versus artificial, public versus private, free versus enslaved. We could see the distinction between "clean" and "dirty" in relation to drug users (and their urine) as an embodiment of the duality in the rhetoric of drugs, as the pharmakon. Derrida argues for a move away from this duality, which has been translated into political regimes of either prohibition or liberalization, when he writes, "A thinking and a politics of this thing called 'drugs' would involve the displacement of these two ideologies at *once* opposed in their common metaphysics" (34).
42. Fraser and valentine, *Substance and Substitution*, 2.
43. Conrad and Schneider, *Deviance and Medicalization*.
44. SAMHSA, "Treatment Episodes Data Set (TEDS) Highlights."
45. Peyton and Gossweiler, "Treatment Services in Adult Drug Courts."
46. NIDA, "Thirteen Principles of Drug Addiction Treatment," 5.
47. Fox, "Medicalization and Demedicalization of American Society."

Notes to Chapter 5

1. Satel, "Drug Treatment."
2. Many of the drug court advocates I spoke with mentioned, and much of the drug court literature refers to, popular public support for coerced drug treatment and drug courts. I was unable to locate any opinion polls that asked respondents specifically about coerced drug treatment. However, I did find

one survey that touched on the topic of rehabilitation. The Pew Research Center reports that, as of 2003 (the most recent year they asked this question of respondents), 72% of Americans "think the criminal justice system should try to rehabilitate criminals and not just punish them," and that, overall, "large majorities of both Democrats and Republicans endorse the idea of rehabilitating criminals, as well as punishing them" (Pew Research Center, "2004 Political Landscape," 75, 76).

3. Harrison and Scarpitti, "Introduction," 1447.
4. Ibid.
5. Satel, "Observational Study of Courtroom Dynamics in Selected Drug Courts," 71.
6. Ibid.
7. Butts, "Introduction," 121.
8. Fox, *Bridging the Gap*, 6.
9. Berman et al., *A Problem-Solving Revolution*.
10. Satel, "Observational Study of Courtroom Dynamics in Selected Drug Courts," 59.
11. NDCI, "Critical Need for Jail as a Sanction in the Drug Court Model."
12. One training document I received from an interviewee cited behavioral studies of rats to explain the psychological principles underlying a system of sanctions and rewards to motivate behavior change in humans.
13. Harrison and Scarpitti, "Introduction," 1447.
14. NADCP, "Defining Drug Courts," 23–25.
15. Olson et al., "Implementing the Key Components of Specialized Treatment Courts," 181.
16. Ibid., 182.
17. Ibid.
18. Satel, "Observational Study of Courtroom Dynamics in Selected Drug Courts," 58.
19. Ibid, 67.
20. Judge Leslie Leach as quoted in Fisler et al., "Edited Transcript," 29–30.
21. Carol Shapiro as quoted in ibid., 23.
22. Butts, "Introduction," 121.
23. Ibid., 123.
24. Berman and Feinblatt, "Judges and Problem-Solving Courts," 5.
25. As quoted in Fox and Berman, "Going to Scale," 9.
26. DCPO, "Defining Drug Courts."
27. As quoted in Fisler et al., "Edited Transcript," 18.
28. DCPO, "Defining Drug Courts."
29. Freeman-Wilson, "Testimony of the National Association of Drug Court Professionals National Drug Court Institute," 5.

30. See, for example, Berman et al., *Problem-Solving Revolution*.
31. Berman and Anderson, "Drugs, Courts, and Neighborhoods," 14.
32. Michelle Sviridoff as quoted in Fisler et al., "Edited Transcript," 17.
33. Berman, "Redefining Criminal Courts," 1314.
34. Ibid.
35. Satel, "Drug Treatment."
36. Satel, "For Addicts, Firm Hand Can Be the Best Medicine."
37. John Marr as quoted in Fisler et al., "Edited Transcript," 13–14.
38. Fox and Berman, "Going to Scale," 4.
39. In *Rules of the Sociological Method*, Emile Durkheim explains that social facts are external to us and imposed through coercion, and yet we think they are internal to us and often "natural" expressions of the way things are. Addiction is a powerful social fact; the truth of addiction is coerced on us in a variety of ways that inform how we act on this social fact, seen as a natural rather than socially constructed phenomenon.
40. Garriott, *Policing Methamphetamine*.
41. Derrida, "Rhetoric of Drugs."
42. Valverde, *Disease of the Will*; Vrecko, "'Civilizing Technologies' and the Control of Deviance."
43. In *Governing the Soul*, Nikolas Rose argues that the "psy disciplines"— psychiatry and psychology—serve as a mode of governing at a distance through the creation of a subjectivity based on the normalizing ideas inherent in the psychological disciplines. Psychology and psychiatry provide the language that the state harnesses to make its citizens conform in ways that directly serve the political interests of order; they serve as a scientific and rational way to ensure conformity. They establish norms of psychological health that serve to guide the conduct of individuals and provide the language and strategies for acting on bodies to help them achieve health and happiness. They link to discourses of the responsibility of individuals to achieve this health precisely because the means to normalcy are at their disposal. They rely on the notion of "potential" as a project we are compelled to work toward; normative judgment acts as the coercive mechanism that inspires us to manage ourselves through the expert techniques available. Psychiatry and psychology constitute a political rationale, demanding that individuals govern themselves so that the state doesn't have to directly with force and overt coercion. People discipline themselves through a logic of personal empowerment and betterment that is seen not only as their right but also as their responsibility.

    According to this theory of "governmentality," norms of psychological and physical health are achieved through persuasion rather than overt coercion. One of the accomplishments of the science of subjectivity, Rose argues, is an ideology where people are "free" to regulate themselves. However, with drug courts and other coerced sanctions that rely on psychological theories of deviance, health is literally coerced onto people. They don't choose but rather are forced into sobriety and psychological "health" in a system where they have lost their "freedom" (meaning, in part, the pursuit of the regulated and disciplined life) because of their failure to conform.

44. O'Malley and Valverde in "Pleasure, Freedom, and Drugs" detail how "moderation" is a hallmark of liberal governance; "risk" becomes an important ideological tool serving to remind people of the link between "moderation" and "rationality." Pleasure is assigned to those who can consume drugs moderately; pain is assigned to those who have succumbed to risks. As they write, "Freedom of choice has a rather sharp edge, in which individuals are rendered more personally responsible for governance of harm," the sharp edge being "exposure to pain and punishment" (39). Garriott, in *Policing Methamphetamine*, highlights how "narcopolitics" engages with the idea of "threat" so that drug control is about preventing future harm rather than solely punishing past illicit drug activity. The "threat" and "risk" of future drug use are directly invoked as justifications for therapeutic sanctions and their expansion into increasing aspects of defendants' lives.

45. Rose, "Neurochemical Self and Its Anomalies."

46. Valverde, *Disease of the Will*.

47. Lieupo and Weinstein, "Ballot Initiatives"; Marlowe et al., "Judge Is a Key Component of Drug Court."

48. NIDA, "Thirteen Principles of Drug Addiction Treatment," 5.

49. Berman and Feinblatt, "Judges and Problem-Solving Courts."

50. Ibid.

Notes to Chapter 6

1. Fox, *Bridging the Gap*, 1.

2. NADCP, "From the Chief Executive's Desk," 1.

3. Fox and Berman, "Going to Scale," 4.

4. Fox, *Bridging the Gap*.

5. As quoted in Fox and Huddleston, "Drug Courts in the U.S.," 10.

6. Marlowe, "Drug Court Efficacy versus Effectiveness," 2.

7. Cheesman et al., "Developing Statewide Performance Measure for Drug Courts," 3.

8. Roman, "Accreditation Key to Creating the Next Generation of Drug Courts," 2.

9. As quoted in Fox, *Bridging the Gap*, 11.

10. Ibid.

11. Ibid., 7.

12. Platt, *Child Savers*, 43.

13. Ibid., 44–45.

14. Osher and Levine, "Navigating the Mental Health Maze."

15. Thompson et al., "Improving Responses to People with Mental Illnesses," 9.

16. NDCI, "Ten Guiding Principles of DWI Courts."

17. AMS, "SCRAMx," http://alcoholmonitoring.com/ams_files/resources/SCRAMxdatasheet.pdf.

18. Belson, "New York Gambling Treatment Court Stresses Help."

19. SAMHSA, "Treatment Episodes Data Set (TEDS) Highlights."

20. BJA, "Juvenile Drug Court," 6.

21. Paik, *Discretionary Justice,* 4.

22. Ibid., 9.

23. Butts and Roman, "Introduction," 8.

24. Brenhouse and Andersen, "Delayed Extinction and Stronger Reinstatement of Cocaine Conditioned Place Preference in Adolescent Rats."

25. Join Together, "Animal Study Hints at Greater Teen Susceptibility to Addiction," http://www.drugfree.org/join-together/addiction/animal-study-hints-at-greater.

26. American Psychological Association, "Rat Study Suggests Why Teens Get Hooked on Cocaine More Easily Than Adults," http://www.biologynews.net/archives/2008/04/21/rat_study_suggests_why_teens_get_hooked_on_cocaine_more_easily_than_adults.html.

27. OJP, "Juvenile and Family Drug Courts," 1.

28. Ibid., 7.

29. BJA, "Juvenile Drug Court," 7.

30. Ibid., 8.

31. Ibid., 44.

32. Ibid., 22.

33. As quoted in Paik, *Discretionary Justice,* 101.

34. BJA, "Juvenile Drug Court," 20.

35. Ibid., 54.

36. Ibid.

37. Ibid., 8.

38. Ibid., 17.

39. Ibid., 7.

40. Gorski, *Disciplinary Revolution.*

41. Foucault, *Discipline and Punish.*

42. Ibid., 129.

43. Deleuze, "Postscript on the Societies of Control."

44. Lupton, *Imperative of Health*; Rose, *Governing the Soul.*

45. SAMHSA, "Results from the 2006 National Survey on Drug Use and Health"; Fellner, "Targeting Blacks"; King, "Disparity by Geography."

Notes to the Conclusion

1. Perez Hilton, "Redmond O'Neal Arrested! Again! While Still in Court-Mandated Rehab!" http://perezhilton. com/2010-01-05-redmond-arrested-again-while-still-in-rehab.

2. Garriott in *Policing Methamphetamine* argues that one of the triumphs of "narcopolitics" is the linking of drugs and crime so that it's almost impossible to talk about drugs without the assumption that they are the cause of crime. Of course, the link between drugs and crime was made explicit when drugs were criminalized. As Acker in *Creating the American Junkie* points out, this criminalization is an artifact of increasing regimes of drug prohibition that in essence turned some drug users into criminals overnight.

3. Zinberg in *Drug, Set, and Setting* argues that most drug users, even those we deem addicts, control their drug use in some way. An important factor in this control is the setting where people learn how to act on and consume drugs, and, importantly, where they learn how not to act when using a certain drug. The setting, rather than enabling drug use, can act as a protective factor, inhibiting harms while teaching drug users how to maximize their safe consumption of mind-altering substances. Zinberg argues that drug prohibition can make drug use unsafe because it inhibits the development of formalized settings for drug use, compelling drug users, because of fear of detection, to use drugs alone or clandestinely.

4. O'Malley and Valverde, "Pleasure, Freedom, and Drugs."

5. Ibid.; valentine and Fraser, "Trauma, Damage, and Pleasure"; Holt and Treloar, "Pleasure and Drugs."

6. Levi and Appel, "Collateral Consequences"; Tiger and Finkelstein, "Public Policy Context of Drug Use in New York City."

7. Howard Becker in *Outsiders* articulates the importance of the labeling theory of deviance—things are deviant that are labeled as such. His perspective was important for opening up the idea that deviance was relative and the labeling of someone as deviant was a political act and an act of power. Through the process of labeling, the rulebreaker's "master status" becomes their deviance so that their identity is seen through this framework. Thus we call someone a "murderer" who might have spent only a moment actually killing someone. Once they commit this deviant act, however, their past, present, and future identities are read through their master deviant status.

8. Granfield and Cloud, "Elephant That No One Sees"; Granfield and Cloud, *Coming Clean*; Reinarman et al., *Cocaine Changes*.

9. Granfield and Cloud, "Elephant That No One Sees."
10. King, "Disparity by Geography."
11. NIDA, "About Drug Abuse," http://www.nida.nih.gov/about/welcome/aboutdrugabuse/.
12. As quoted in Daly, "Psychiatric News."
13. NIDA, "Info and Facts," http://www.nida.nih.gov/Infofacts/treatmeth.html.
14. Lupton, *Imperative of Health.*
15. Ibid.; Petersen and Lupton, *New Public Health.* Lupton and Peterson, scholars of "the new public health," argue that the personal responsibility for illness that attends public health discourses is accompanied by an emphasis on the lifestyle choices people make that are seen to bring about their illnesses. As increasing aspects of human life are defined in terms of health and illness, the responsibility of individuals to prevent these conditions, and their social costs, is increasing as well. The "enterprising and entrepreneurial self" takes positive action to pursue health, in part because of the negative moral judgment that accompanies illness and the social praise that encourages the outward pursuit of health (Petersen and Lupton, *New Public Health,* 69). Addiction, as an illness that requires the addict's willpower to cure, sits between public health and medicine, if cure is defined as abstinence. The addict's choices are directly implicated in the disease's progression and cure. The new public health emphasizes the diffuse personal responsibility for health disseminated by, largely, the health promotion discourse. Yet social institutions help to enact the surveillance necessary to monitor health and to provide the impetus, often voluntary but not always, to ensure people actively pursue their health in the face of disease and illness.
16. Petersen and Lupton, *New Public Health.*
17. Levine and Small, "Marijuana Arrest Crusade."
18. Dolan et al., "Drug Consumption Facilities in Europe and the Establishment of Supervised Injection Centres in Australia."
19. UHRI, "Findings from the Evaluation of Vancouver's Pilot Medically Supervised Safer Injection Facility."
20. Ibid.
21. Critiques of harm reduction have emerged that focus on it as an ancillary mode of governance in neoliberal regimes. O'Malley and Valverde in "Pleasure, Freedom, and Drugs" note the absence of pleasure in harm reduction discourse, which assumes a "neutrality" when discussing drug use but that really serves to underscore it as a harmful activity whose negative consequences should be managed by the individual, seen as "at risk," because of their drug use, without harm reduction interventions. Moore in "Governing Street-Based Injection Drugs Users" argues that harm reduction tends to

focus on the individual factors that produce risk among habitual substance users, and in doing so ignores the "macro factors" of "risk environments."

Fischer and his coauthors in "Drug Use, Risk, and Urban Order" focus on supervised injection sites as a form of "post-welfare governmentality," where "disorderly" drug users are moved from the center of urban spaces to a "ghettoized" periphery as a way of "purifying public spaces" for the rational and reasonable inhabitants of gentrification. Harm reduction here is a form of "risk management" meant to promote order through the social control and surveillance of injection drug users and their marginalization into specific spaces, where they can inject drugs outside the public eye. Here, drug users are not viewed as part of the public but rather a sort of threat to it.

These critiques of harm reduction discourse and practice do the important work of showing how difficult it is to talk about drug use in a non-pathologizing framework, even when the goal of harm reduction programs is often to reframe the discussion of substance use away from one dominated by law enforcement paradigms.

22. Moynihan, "For Drugs Users, Coalition Serves as Voice in Albany."
23. Szalavitz, "Addiction Files."
24. Ibid., 3.
25. Derrida, "Rhetoric of Drugs."
26. King and Pasquarella, "Drug Courts"; Orr et al., "America's-Problem Solving Courts."
27. O'Hear, "Rethinking Drug Courts."
28. Orr et al., "America's Problem-Solving Courts."
29. O'Hear, "Rethinking Drug Courts"; Orr et al., "America's Problem-Solving Courts."
30. Rothman, *Conscience and Convenience*, 10.

Notes to the Appendix

1. Berger and Luckmann, *Social Construction of Reality*.
2. Fitzpatrick, "Drug Courts Seek to Broaden Influence through Model Law."
3. Berger and Luckmann, *Social Construction of Reality*.
4. Fox and Wolf, "Future of Drug Courts."
5. Abbott, *System of Professions*, 57.
6. Alford, *Health Care Politics*.
7. Huddleston et al., "Painting the Current Picture."
8. Berman and Anderson, "Drugs, Courts, and Neighborhoods."
9. Ibid.; Satel, "Drug Treatment."
10. See, for example, Marlowe et al., "Judge Is a Key Component of Drug Court."

11. Maxwell, *Qualitative Research Design*, 70.
12. Bernard, *Research Methods in Anthropology.*
13. Ibid., 97.
14. Marshall and Rossman, *Designing Qualitative Research*, 83.
15. I am thankful to my friend and colleague Richard Elovitch for coining this phrase and helping me articulate my thoughts about the effects—both positive and negative—of associating anonymity with institutionally powerful actors.
16. Maxwell, *Qualitative Research Design*, 33.
17. Alford, *Craft of Inquiry*, 29.
18. Ibid., 29.
19. Ibid., 42.

Bibliography

Abbott, Andrew. 1988. *The System of Professions: An Essay on the Division of Expert Labor*. Chicago: University of Chicago Press.

Acker, Caroline Jean. 2002. *Creating the American Junkie: Addiction Research in the Classic Era of Narcotic Control*. Baltimore: Johns Hopkins University Press.

Alford, Robert R. 1975. *Health Care Politics: Ideological and Interest Group Barriers to Reform*. Chicago: University of Chicago Press.

———. 1998. *The Craft of Inquiry: Theories, Methods, Evidence*. New York: Oxford University Press.

Armstrong, Elizabeth M. 2003. *Conceiving Risk, Bearing Responsibility: Fetal Alcohol Syndrome and the Diagnosis of a Moral Disorder*. Baltimore: Johns Hopkins University Press.

Attewell, Paul, and Dean R. Gerstein. 1979. "Government Policy and Local Practice." *American Sociological Review* 44:311–327.

Becker, Howard. 1963. *Outsiders: Studies in the Sociology of Deviance*. New York: Free Press.

Beckett, Katherine. 1999. *Making Crime Pay: Law and Order in Contemporary American Politics*. New York: Oxford University Press.

Beckett, Katherine, and Bruce Western. 2001. "Governing Social Marginality: Welfare, Incarceration, and the Transformation of State Policy." Pp. 35–50 in *Mass Imprisonment: Social Causes and Consequences*, edited by David Garland. Thousand Oaks, CA: Sage.

Belenko, S. 1998. "Research on Drug Courts: A Critical Review." *National Drug Court Institute Review* 1:1–42.

Belson, Ken. 2007. "New York Gambling Treatment Court Stresses Help." *The New York Times*.

Berger, Peter L., and Thomas Luckmann. 1966. *The Social Construction of Reality: A Treatise in the Sociology of Knowledge*. New York: Anchor.

Berman, Greg. 2004. "Redefining Criminal Courts: Problem-Solving and the Meaning of Justice." *American Criminal Law Review* 41:1313–1319.

Berman, Greg, and David Anderson. 1999. "Drugs, Courts, and Neighborhoods." New York: Center for Court Innovation.

Berman, Greg, and John Feinblatt. 2002. "Judges and Problem-Solving Courts." New York: Center for Court Innovation.

———. 2005. *Good Courts: The Case for Problem-Solving Justice*. New York: New Press.

Berman, Greg, Aubrey Fox, and Robert V. Wolf, eds. 2004. *A Problem-Solving*

Revolution: Making Change Happen in State Courts. New York: Center for Court Innovation.

Bernard, H. Russell. 1995. *Research Methods in Anthropology: Qualitative and Quantitative Approaches.* Walnut Creek, CA: AltaMira Press.

Best, Joel. 1990. *Threatened Children: Rhetoric and Concern about Child-Victims.* Chicago: University of Chicago Press.

BJA (Bureau of Justice Assistance). 2003. "Juvenile Drug Courts: Strategies in Practice." Washington, DC: Bureau of Justice Assistance, Office of Justice Programs, U.S. Department of Justice.

BJS (Bureau of Justice Statistics). 2007. "Probation and Parole in the United States, 2007." Washington, DC: Bureau of Justice Statistics.

———. 2008. "Correctional Population in the United States, Annual Prisoners in 2008." Washington, DC: Bureau of Justice Statistics.

Bortner, M. A. 1982. *Inside a Juvenile Court: The Tarnished Ideal of Individualized Justice.* New York: New York University Press.

Bourgois, Philippe. 2000. "Disciplining Addictions: The Bio-politics of Methadone and Heroin in the United States." *Culture, Medicine, and Psychiatry* 24:165–195.

Brenhouse, Heather C., and Susan L. Andersen. 2008. "Delayed Extinction and Stronger Reinstatement of Cocaine Conditioned Place Preference in Adolescent Rats, Compared to Adults." *Behavioral Neuroscience* 122:460–465.

Burns, Stacy Lee, and Mark Peyrot. 2003. "Tough Love: Nurturing and Coercing Responsibility and Recovery in California Drug Courts." *Social Problems* 50:416–438.

Butts, Jeffrey A. 2001. "Introduction: Problem-Solving Courts." *Law and Policy* 23:121–124.

Cheesman, Fred, Dawn M. Rubio, and Richard Van Duizend. 2004. "Developing Statewide Performance Measures for Drug Courts." *Statewide Technical Assistance Bulletin, National Center for State Courts* 2:1–8.

Christie, Nils. 1998. "Changes in Penal Values." Pp. 105–116 in *The Sociology of Punishment: Socio-structural Perspectives,* edited by Dario Melossi. Brookfield, VT: Ashgate.

Cissner, Amanda, and Michael Rempel. 2005. "The State of Drug Court Research: Moving Beyond 'Do They Work?'" New York: Center for Court Innovation.

Clarke, Adele E., Laura Mamo, Jennifer R. Fishman, Janet K. Shim, and Jennifer Ruth Fosket. 2003. "Biomedicalization: Technoscientific Transformations of Health, Illness, and U.S. Biomedicine." *American Sociological Review* 68:161–194.

Clarkson, Chris, and Rod Morgan, eds. 1995. *The Politics of Sentencing Reform.* Oxford: Clarendon Press.

Conrad, Peter. 1992. "Medicalization and Social Control." *Annual Review of Sociology* 18:209–232.

Conrad, Peter, and Joseph W. Schneider. 1992. *Deviance and Medicalization: From Badness to Sickness*. Philadelphia: Temple University Press.

COPS (Community Oriented Policing Services). 2009. "One-on-One with ONDCP Director Gil Kerlikowske." *Community Policing Dispatch* 2: http://www.cops.usdoj.gov/html/dispatch/index.asp.

Daly, Rich. 2007. "Psychiatric News." *American Psychiatric Association* 42:14.

DCPO (Drug Courts Program Office). 1997. "Defining Drug Courts: The Key Components." Washington, DC: U.S. Department of Justice, Office of Justice Programs, Drug Courts Program Office.

Deleuze, Gilles. 1992. "Postscript on the Societies of Control." *October* 59:3–7.

Derrida, Jacques. 2003. "The Rhetoric of Drugs." Pp. 19–43 in *High Culture: Reflections on Addiction and Modernity*, edited by Anne Alexander and Mark S. Roberts. Albany: State University of New York Press.

Dolan, Kate, Jo Kimber, Craig Fry, and John Fitzgerald. 2000. "Drug Consumption Facilities in Europe and the Establishment of Supervised Injection Centres in Australia." *Drug and Alcohol Review* 19:337–347.

Drug Courts Program Office. 2000. "About the Drug Courts Program Office: Fact Sheet." Washington, DC: U.S. Department of Justice, Office of Justice Programs.

Drug Policy Alliance. 2011. "Drug Courts Are Not the Answer: Toward a Health-Centered Approach to Drug Use." New York: Drug Policy Alliance.

Durkheim, Emile. 1982. *The Rules of the Sociological Method*. New York: Free Press.

Eckholm, Erik. 2008. "Innovative Courts Give Some Addicts the Chance to Straighten Out." *The New York Times*.

Erikson, Kai T. 1966. *Wayward Puritans: A Study in the Sociology of Deviance*. New York: Macmillan.

Feeley, M. M., and J. Simon. 1992. "The New Penology: Notes on the Emerging Strategies of Corrections and Its Implications." *Criminology* 30:449–474.

Feld, Barry. 1999. *Bad Kids: Race and the Transformation of the Juvenile Court*. New York: Oxford University Press.

Fellner, Jamie. 2008. "Targeting Blacks: Drug Law Enforcement and Race in the United States." New York: Human Rights Watch.

Finkelstein, Katherine E. 2000. "New York to Offer Most Addicts Treatment Instead of Jail Terms." *The New York Times*.

Fischer, Benedikt, Sarah Turnbull, Blake Poland, and Emma Haydon. 2004. "Drug Use, Risk, and Urban Order: Examining Supervised Injection Sites (SISs) as 'Governmentality.'" *International Journal of Drug Policy* 15:357–365.

Fisler, Carol, Greg Berman, and Aubrey Fox. 2001. "Edited Transcript: Risks and Rewards: Drug Courts and Community Reintegration." *National Drug Court Institute Review* 3:3–33.

Fitzpatrick, Colleen. 2004. "Drug Courts Seek to Broaden Influence through Model Law." *Alcoholism and Drug Abuse Weekly* 3:1–33.

Foucault, Michel. 1995 [1975]. *Discipline and Punish: The Birth of the Prison.* New York: Vintage.

Fox, Aubrey, ed. 2004. "Bridging the Gap: Researchers, Practitioners, and the Future of Drug Courts." New York: Center for Court Innovation.

Fox, Aubrey, and Greg Berman. 2002. "Going to Scale: A Conversation about the Future of Drug Courts." *Court Review* 39:4–13.

Fox, Aubrey, and Robert V. Wolf. 2004. "The Future of Drug Courts: How States Are Mainstreaming the Drug Court Model." New York: Center for Court Innovation.

Fox, Carson, and C. West Huddleston. 2003. "Drug Courts in the U.S." *Issues of Democracy* 8:13–19.

Fox, Renee C. 2001. "The Medicalization and Demedicalization of American Society." Pp. 414–418 in *The Sociology of Health and Illness: Critical Perspectives,* 6th ed., edited by Peter Conrad. New York: Worth.

Fraser, Suzanne, and kylie valentine. 2008. *Substance and Substitution: Methadone Subjects in Liberal Societies.* New York: Palgrave Macmillan.

Freeman-Wilson, Karen. 2004. "Testimony of the National Association of Drug Court Professionals National Drug Court Institute." In *Oversight Hearing: "Measuring the Effectiveness of Drug Addiction Treatment."* Washington, DC: U.S. House of Representatives, Committee on Government Reform, Subcommittee on Criminal Justice, Drug Policy, and Human Resources.

Friedland, Roger, and Robert Alford. 1991. "Bringing Society Back In: Symbols, Practices, and Institutional Contradictions." Pp. 232–263 in *The New Institutionalism in Organizational Analysis,* edited by W. W. Powell and P. J. DiMaggio. Chicago: University of Chicago Press.

GAO (Government Accountability Office). 2005. "Adult Drug Courts: Evidence Indicates Recidivism Reductions and Mixed Results for Other Outcomes." Washington, DC: U.S. Government Accountability Office.

Garland, David. 1990. *Punishment and Modern Society.* Chicago: University of Chicago Press.

———. 2001. *The Culture of Control: Crime and Social Order in Contemporary Society.* Chicago: University of Chicago Press.

Garriott, William. 2011. *Policing Methamphetamine: Narcopolitics in Rural America.* New York: New York University Press.

Gillie, Nick, and C. West Huddleston. 2009. "'All Rise!': A Better Way of Justice Is Now in Session." *Huffington Post.*

Global Commission on Drugs. 2011. "War on Drugs: Report of the Global Commission on Drug Policy." Rio de Janeiro: Global Commission on Drugs.

Goffman, Erving. 1963. *Stigma: Notes on the Management of a Spoiled Identity*. New York: Simon and Schuster.

Goldkamp, John S., Michael D. White, and Jennifer B. Robinson. 2001. "Do Drug Courts Work? Getting inside the Drug Court Black Box." *Journal of Drug Issues* 31:27–72.

Gorski, Philip S. 2003. *The Disciplinary Revolution: Calvinism and the Rise of the State in Early Modern Europe*. Chicago: University of Chicago Press.

Granfield, R., and W. Cloud. 1996. "The Elephant That No One Sees: Natural Recovery among Middle-Class Addicts." *Journal of Drug Issues* 26:45–61.

———. 1999. *Coming Clean: Overcoming Addiction without Treatment*. New York: New York University Press.

Gusfield, Joseph R. 1981. *The Culture of Public Problems: Drinking–Driving and the Symbolic Order*. Chicago: University of Chicago Press.

———. 1986. *Symbolic Crusade: Status Politics and the American Temperance Movement*. Chicago: University of Illinois Press.

———. 1996. *Contested Meanings: The Construction of Alcohol Problems*. Madison: University of Wisconsin Press.

———. 1997. "Alcohol in America: The Entangled Frames of Health and Morality." Pp. 201–229 in *Morality and Health*, edited by Allan M. Brandt and Paul Rozin. New York: Routledge.

———. 2003. "A Journey with Symbolic Interaction." *Symbolic Interaction* 26:119–139.

Hacking, Ian. 1990. *The Taming of Chance*. Cambridge: Cambridge University Press.

Harrison, Lana D., and Frank R. Scarpitti. 2002. "Introduction: Progress and Issues in Drug Treatment Courts." *Substance Use and Misuse* 37:1441–1467.

Holt, Martin, and Carla Treloar. 2008. "Pleasure and Drugs: Editorial." *International Journal of Drug Policy* 19:349–352.

Hook, Derek. 2001. "Discourse, Knowledge, Materiality, History: Foucault and Discourse Analysis." *Theory and Psychology* 11:521–547.

Huddleston, C. West, and Douglas Marlowe. 2011. "Painting the Current Picture: A National Report Card on Drug Courts and Other Problem Solving Court Programs in the United States." Alexandria, VA: National Drug Court Institute.

Huddleston, C. West, Douglas Marlowe, and Rachel Casebolt. 2008. "Painting the Current Picture: A National Report Card on Drug Courts and Other Problem Solving Court Programs in the United States." Alexandria, VA: National Drug Court Institute.

Jensen, Elizabeth. 2007. "Facing 'Things That Destroy Your Life.'" *The New York Times*.

Johnson, Carrie. 2009. "Choice of Drug Czar Indicates Focus on Treatment Not Jail." *The Washington Post.*

Kassebaum, G., and D. K. Okamoto. 2001. "The Drug Court as a Sentencing Model." *Journal of Contemporary Criminal Justice* 17:89–104.

Keane, Helen, and Kelly Hamill. 2010. "Variations in Addiction: The Molecular and the Moral in Neuroscience and Pain Medicine." *BioSocieties* 5:52–69.

King, Ryan. 2008. "Disparity by Geography: The War on Drugs in America's Cities." Washington, DC: The Sentencing Project.

King, Ryan, and Jill Pasquarella. 2009. "Drug Courts: A Review of the Evidence." Washington, DC: The Sentencing Project.

Klein, Richard. 2010. "What Is Health and How Do You Get It?" Pp. 15–25 in *Against Health: How Health Became the New Morality,* edited by Jonathan M. Metzl and Anna Kirkland. New York: New York University Press.

Kolbert, Elizabeth. 1997. "A Drug Court Takes a Risk to Aid Addicts." *The New York Times.*

Kupchik, Aaron. 2006. *Judging Juveniles: Prosecuting Adolescents in Adult and Juvenile Courts.* New York: New York University Press.

Lay, Donald P. 2004. "Rehab Justice." *The New York Times.*

Levi, Robin, and Judith Appel. 2003. "Collateral Consequences: Denial of Basic Social Services Based upon Drug Use." Berkeley: Drug Policy Alliance.

Levine, Harry G. 1978. "The Discovery of Addiction: Changing Conceptions of Habitual Drunkenness in America." *Journal of Studies on Alcohol* 39:143–174.

Levine, Harry, and Deborah Peterson Small. 2008. "Marijuana Arrest Crusade: Racial Bias and Policy in New York City, 1997–2007." New York: New York Civil Liberties Union.

Lieupo, Kelly, and Susan P. Weinstein. 2004. "Ballot Initiatives: Wolves in Sheep's Clothing." *Drug Court Review* 4:51–66.

Lupton, Deborah. 1995. *The Imperative of Health: Public Health and the Regulated Body.* Thousand Oaks, CA: Sage.

Lynch, Mona. 2001. "Rehabilitation as Rhetoric: The Idea of Reformation in Contemporary Parole Discourses and Practices." *Punishment and Society* 2:40–65.

Marlowe, D. B., D. S. Festinger, and P. A. Lee. 2004. "The Judge Is a Key Component of Drug Court." *National Drug Court Institute Review* 4:1–34.

Marlowe, Douglas B. 2004. "Drug Court Efficacy versus Effectiveness." Boston: Join Together.

Maron, Dina Fine. 2009. "Courting Drug-Policy Reform: A Bipartisan Drug Policy 20 Years in the Making?" *Newsweek.*

Marshall, Catherine, and Gretchen B. Rossman. 1995. *Designing Qualitative Research.* Thousand Oaks, CA: Sage.

Martinson, Robert. 1974. "What Works? Questions and Answers about Prison Reform." *The Public Interest* 10:22–54.

Mauer, Marc. 1995. *Malign Neglect: Race, Crime, and Punishment in America*. New York: Oxford University Press.

———. 2001. "The Causes and Consequences of Prison Growth in the United States." Pp. 4–14 in *Mass Imprisonment: Social Causes and Consequences*, edited by David Garland. Thousand Oaks, CA: Sage.

Maxwell, Joseph. 1996. *Qualitative Research Design: An Interactive Approach*. Thousand Oaks, CA: Sage.

May, Carl. 2001. "Pathology, Identity, and the Social Construction of Alcohol Dependence." *Sociology* 35:385–401.

Moore, David. 2004. "Governing Street-Based Injection Drug Users: A Critique of Heroin Overdose Prevention in Australia." *Social Science and Medicine* 59:1547–1557.

Moynihan, Colin. 2010. "For Drug Users, Coalition Serves as Voice in Albany." *The New York Times*.

Musto, David. 1999. *The American Disease: Origins of Narcotic Control*. New York: Oxford University Press.

NADCP (National Association of Drug Court Professionals). 1997. "Defining Drug Courts: The Key Components." Alexandria: National Association of Drug Court Professionals, Drug Court Standards Committee.

———. 2007. "From the Chief Executive's Desk." *NADCP News*. Alexandria, VA: National Association of Drug Court Professionals.

———. 2009. "All Rise." *All Rise: Restoring Lives, Reuniting Families, and Making Communities Safer* 1:3.

NDCI (National Drug Court Institute). n.d. "The Ten Guiding Principles of DWI Courts." Alexandria, VA: National Drug Court Institute.

———. 2000. "The Critical Need for Jail as a Sanction in the Drug Court Model." *Drug Court Practitioner Fact Sheet* 2:1–4.

Nelkin, Dorothy. 1973. *Methadone Maintenance: A Technological Fix*. New York: George Braziller.

NIDA (National Institutes of Health). 2000 [1999]. "Thirteen Principles of Drug Addiction Treatment: A Research Based Guide." Rockville, MD: U.S. Department of Health and Human Services, National Institutes of Health, National Institute on Drug Abuse.

———. 2007. "Drugs, Brains, and Behavior: The Science of Addiction." Washington, DC: National Institute on Drug Abuse, National Institutes of Health, Department of Health and Human Services.

Nolan, James R. 2001. *Reinventing Justice: The American Drug Court Movement*. Princeton: Princeton University Press.

———. 2002a. "Drug Treatment Courts and the Disease Paradigm." *Substance Use and Misuse* 37:1723–1750.

———. 2002b. "Therapeutic Adjudication." *Society* 39:29–39.

O'Hear, Michael M. 2009. "Rethinking Drug Courts: Restorative Justice as a Response to Racial Injustice." *Stanford Law and Policy Review* 20:101–137.

OJP (Office of Justice Programs). 1998. "Juvenile and Family Drug Courts: An Overview." Washington, DC: Office of Justice Programs Drug Court Clearing House and Technical Assistance Project, American University.

Olson, David E., Arthur J. Lurigio, and Stephanie Albertson. 2001. "Implementing the Key Components of Specialized Treatment Courts: Practice and Policy Considerations." *Law and Policy* 23:171–196.

O'Malley, Pat, and Mariana Valverde. 2004. "Pleasure, Freedom, and Drugs: The Uses of 'Pleasure' in Liberal Governance of Drug and Alcohol Consumption." *Sociology* 38:25–42.

Osher, Fred C., and Irene S. Levine. 2005. "Navigating the Mental Health Maze: A Guide for Court Practitioners." Washington, DC: Bureau of Justice Assistance, Mental Health Courts Program.

Paik, Leslie. 2011. *Discretionary Justice: Looking inside a Juvenile Drug Court*. New Brunswick: Rutgers University Press.

Petersen, Alan, and Deborah Lupton. 1996. *The New Public Health: Health and Self in the Age of Risk*. Thousand Oaks, CA: Sage.

Pew Research Center. 2003. "The 2004 Political Landscape: Evenly Divided and Increasingly Polarized." Washington, DC: Pew Research Center for the People and the Press.

Peyton, E. A., and R. Gossweiler. 2001. "Treatment Services in Adult Drug Courts: Report on the 1999 National Drug Court Treatment Survey." Washington, DC: Drug Courts Program Office, Office of Justice Programs, U.S. Department of Justice.

Piper, Bill. 2010. "Obama's Drug War Budget Looks a Lot Like Bush's." *AlterNet*.

Platt, A. M. 1977. *The Child Savers: The Invention of Delinquency*. Chicago: University of Chicago Press.

Reinarman, Craig. 2005. "Addiction as Accomplishment: The Discursive Construction of Disease." *Addiction Research and Theory* 13:307–320.

Reinarman, Craig, Dan Waldorf, and Sheigla Murphy. 1991. *Cocaine Changes: The Experiences of Using and Quitting*. Philadelphia: Temple University Press.

Rempel, Michael, Dana Fox-Kralstein, and Amanda Cissner. 2004. "Drug Courts an Effective Treatment Alternative." *Criminal Justice* 19:34–38.

Roman, John. 2004. "Accreditation Key to Creating the Next Generation of Drug Courts." Boston: Join Together.

Rose, Nikolas. 1989. *Governing the Soul: The Shaping of the Private Self*. New York: Free Association.

———. 2003. "The Neurochemical Self and Its Anomalies." Pp. 407–437 in *Risk and Morality*, edited by R. Ericson. Toronto: University of Toronto Press.

Rossol, Josh. 2001. "The Medicalization of Deviance as an Interactive Achievement: The Construction of Compulsive Gambling." *Symbolic Interaction* 24:315–341.

Rothman, David. 1990 [1971]. *The Discovery of the Asylum: Social Order and Disorder in the New Republic.* New York: Aldine de Gruyter.

———. 2002 [1980]. *Conscience and Convenience: The Asylum and Its Alternative in Progressive America.* New York: Aldine de Gruyter.

SAMHSA (Substance Abuse and Mental Health Services Administration). 2006. "Characteristics of Young Adult (Aged 18–25) and Youth (Aged 12–17) Admissions: 2004." *The DASIS Report, Issue 21.* Rockville, MD: Substance Abuse and Mental Health Services Administration, Office of Applied Studies.

———. 2007. "Results from the 2006 National Survey on Drug Use and Health: National Findings." Rockville, MD: Substance Abuse and Mental Health Services Administration, Office of Applied Studies.

———. 2008. "Treatment Episodes Data Set (TEDS) Highlights: 2006 National Admissions to Substance Abuse Treatment Services." *DASIS Series: S-40, DHHA Publication No. (SMA) 08-4314.* Rockville, MD: Substance Abuse and Mental Health Services Administration, Office of Applied Studies.

Satel, Sally L. 1998. "Observational Study of Courtroom Dynamics in Selected Drug Courts." *National Drug Court Institute Review* 1:43–72.

———. 2000. "Drug Treatment: The Case for Coercion." *National Drug Court Institute Review* 3:1–23.

———. 2006. "For Addicts, Firm Hand Can Be the Best Medicine." *The New York Times.*

Simon, Jonathan. 1993. *Poor Discipline: Parole and Social Control of the Underclass, 1890–1990.* Chicago: University of Chicago Press.

Snavely, Kathleen R. 2000. "The Critical Need for Jail as a Sanction in the Drug Court Model." *Drug Court Practitioner Fact Sheet.* Alexandria, VA: National Drug Court Institute.

Sparks, Richard. 2003. "State Punishment in Advanced Capitalist Countries." Pp. 19–44 in *Punishment and Social Control,* edited by Thomas G. Blomberg and Stanley Cohen. Hawthorne, NY: Aldine de Gruyter.

Spohn, C., R. K. Piper, T. Martin, and E. D. Frenzel. 2001. "Drug Courts and Recidivism: The Results of an Evaluation Using Two Comparison Groups and Multiple Indicators of Recidivism." *Journal of Drug Issues* 31:149–176.

Swidler, Ann, and Jorge Arditi. 1994. "The New Sociology of Knowledge." *Annual Review of Sociology* 20:305–329.

Szalavitz, Maia. 2010. "Addiction Files: Recovering from Drug Addiction, without Abstinence." *Time: Healthland.* http://healthland.time.com/2010/09/28/addiction-files-recovering-from-drug-addiction-without%C2%A0abstinence/.

Thompson, Michael, Fred Osher, and Denise Tomasini-Joshi. 2007. "Improving

Responses to People with Mental Illnesses: The Essential Elements of a Mental Health Court." New York: Council of State Governments Justice Center.

Tiger, Rebecca. 2011. "Drug Courts and the Logic of Coerced Treatment." *Sociological Forum* 26:169–182.

Tiger, Rebecca, and Ruth Finkelstein. 2002. "The Public Policy Context of Drug Use in New York City." Pp. 255–272 in *Manual for Primary Care Providers: Effectively Caring for Active Substance Users*, edited by Ruth Finkelstein and Sandra Ramos. New York: New York Academy of Medicine.

Tonry, Michael. 1995. *Malign Neglect: Race, Crime, and Punishment in America.* New York: Oxford University Press.

Tunnell, Ken D. 2004. *Pissing on Demand: Workplace Drug Testing and the Rise of the Detox Industry.* New York: New York University Press.

UHRI (Urban Health Research Initiative). 2009. "Findings from the Evaluation of Vancouver's Pilot Medically Supervised Safer Injecting Facility." Vancouver: British Columbia Centre for Excellence in HIV/AIDS.

valentine, kylie, and Suzanne Fraser. 2008. "Trauma, Damage, and Pleasure: Rethinking Problematic Drug Use." *International Journal of Drug Policy* 19:410–416.

Valverde, Mariana. 1998. *Disease of the Will: Alcohol and the Dilemmas of Freedom.* Cambridge: Cambridge University Press.

von Zielbauer, Paul. 2003. "Court Treatment System Is Found to Help Drug Offenders Stay Clean." *The New York Times.*

Vrecko, Scott. 2010. "'Civilizing Technologies' and the Control of Deviance." *BioSocieties* 5:36–51.

Willrich, Michael. 2003. *City of Courts: Socializing Justice in Progressive Era Chicago.* New York: Cambridge University Press.

Wren, Christopher S. 1997. "New Court Lets Drug Addicts Choose Treatment Program Rather Than Jail." *The New York Times.*

Zinberg, Norman. 1984. *Drug, Set and Setting: The Basis for Controlled Intoxicant Use.* New Haven: Yale University Press.

Zola, Irving K. 2001. "Medicine as an Instrument of Social Control." Pp. 404–414 in *The Sociology of Health and Illness: Critical Perspectives*, edited by Peter Conrad. New York: Worth.

Index

About the Author

Rebecca Tiger is Assistant Professor of Sociology at Middlebury College and coeditor of *Bioethical Issues, Sociological Perspectives.*